Off the Map

Off the Map

*The Compelling Story of Believers
Who Learned the Power and Love of God
During a Spirit-led Five Year Journey*

SANDY ROSEN

© Copyright 2006 - Sandy Rosen

All rights reserved. This book is protected under the copyright laws. This book may not be copied or reprinted for commercial gain or profit. The use of short quotations or occasional page copying for personal or group study is permitted and encouraged. Permission will be granted upon request. Unless otherwise identified, Scripture quotations are from the HOLY BIBLE, NEW INTERNATIONAL VERSION®. NIV®. © Copyright 1973, 1978, 1984 by International Bible Society. Used by permission of Zondervan Publishing House. All rights reserved. Please note that Destiny Image Europe's publishing style capitalizes certain pronouns in Scripture that refer to the Father, Son, and Holy Spirit, and may differ from some Bible publishers' styles.

Take note that the name satan and related names are not capitalized. We choose not to acknowledge him, even to the point of violating grammatical rules.

DESTINY IMAGE® EUROPE
Via Maiella, 1
66020 San Giovanni Teatino (Ch) - Italy

ISBN 10: 88-89127-34-1
ISBN 13: 978 88-89127-34-6

For Worldwide Distribution. Printed in the U.S.A.

1 2 3 4 5 6 7 8/10 09 08 07 06

This book and all other Destiny Image Europe books are available at Christian bookstores and distributors worldwide.

To order products, or for any other correspondence:

DESTINY IMAGE® EUROPE
Via Acquacorrente, 6
65123 - Pescara - Italy
Tel. +39 085 4716623 - Fax: +39 085 4716622
E-mail: info@eurodestinyimage.com

Or reach us on the Internet:

www.eurodestinyimage.com

Endorsement

Having watched the Rosen's launch their tour from my little town of Aldergrove, I was thrilled to finally see an account of the whole faith-journey across Canada. If you've ever wondered what would happen if you surrendered yourself to simply listening to God and doing what He says, this is the book for you.

Brad Jersak
Pastor of Freshwind Community Fellowship, Abbotsford, Canada
Author of *Can you Hear Me? Tuning In To the God Who Speaks*

Table of Contents

Foreword 9

CHAPTER 1
Solomon's Colonnade 11

CHAPTER 2
Girding the Vision With Prayer 19

CHAPTER 3
Going With Nothing 31

CHAPTER 4
Standing Between God and Man—
Worship, Evangelism, and Intercession 41

CHAPTER 5
Waiting for God 51

CHAPTER 6
Discovering the Power of the Name of Jesus 59

CHAPTER 7
Bringing Healing into History 67

CHAPTER 8
That They May Be One 75

CHAPTER 9
For Love of God and Neighbor 85

CHAPTER 10
Life in Community 91

CHAPTER 11
Overcoming and Battling 99

CHAPTER 12
"Everywhere We Set Our Foot"—
Claiming the Land 113

CHAPTER 13
Seeing in the Unseen 123

CHAPTER 14
The Gift of Our Diversity 135

CHAPTER 15
In Hot Water—Baptism and Other
Suspicious Activities 145

CHAPTER 16
I'm the Farmer Now—From Seed to Sowing 153

CHAPTER 17
The Young and the Rest 165

CHAPTER 18
God in the Rearview Mirror 175

APPENDIX
Schedule of Events 183

Foreword

A strange irony is afoot in contemporary churches: we have become wary of people who actually follow Jesus. Those rare folk who take Jesus at face value, with all His stark commands and cryptic stories and disruptive influence, seem to us reckless and capricious, like someone who runs off to join the circus. Somehow, most of us in the church equate Gospel faithfulness with middle-class stability. We think Kingdom righteousness and domestic decency is the exact same thing. Not that decency and stability are bad things; but Jesus had nowhere to lay His head at night. Jesus resorted to tricks with fish to pay His taxes and feed His followers. Jesus sought solitary places and rough company. Jesus had demons running from Him and prostitutes running to Him. Surely not just suburbanites with SUVs and whopping mortgages can lay claim to being His disciples.

I have loved Russ and Sandy Rosen since first I met them—and for many reasons—but maybe most because they are both a rebuke and an inspiration to me. They are those rare folk who take Jesus at face value. And in their case it led them, in a manner of speaking, to join the circus—a five year escapade, exhilarating and grueling all at once, to cross Canada in a convoy of semi-trailers and Winnebagos in order to take the message of God's love to every nook and cranny of the country. On the way, God stretched them, tested them, emptied them, filled them, and used them to heal and to bless. Truly, they and their team, Upstream, were "ambassadors of reconciliation" and "signs and symbols" of the Almighty.

Off The Map is the story of those five years. It is testament of Upstream's stubborn faith and God's enduring, abiding faithfulness. It is a diary, psalm-like, of fear and doubt and hope and wonder, and an anthem of the ways God spills His glory in clay pots.

The movie *Hidalgo* is about Frank Hopkins and his Mustang horse that won a race across the Arabian Desert. In one scene, someone asks Frank how he managed to tame Hidalgo.

"I didn't," Frank says.

I picture someone asking God, "How did you tame the Rosens?"

"I didn't," He says.

Read this book only if you've become too tame, too settled, and long to feel again the wind in your face.

Mark Buchanan
Pastor, New Life Community Church,
Duncan, British Columbia, Canada
Author, *Your God Is Too Safe, The Holy Wild, and The Rest of God*

Chapter 1

Solomon's Colonnade

I stood transfixed as they began to file into the Plaza of Nations, my eyes now brimming with tears. Our city had never witnessed anything like it before and its significance was now deeply affecting my already stirred heart. There they were, 15,000 of them, Christians of every sort, all gathering under the glass canopy originally erected for Expo '86—Anglicans, Baptists, Catholics, Mennonites, Pentecostals, Presbyterians, Vineyard—churches that have typically had little to do with one another, all expressing their love and praise for God with one voice. This, the first city-wide interchurch worship and proclamation event that our city had ever experienced, had me completely undone.

I was looking in the rearview mirror of history to a glorious time when the people of God were experiencing a vitality and appeal that continually attracted new people.

> *Every day they continued to meet together in the temple courts (Solomon's Colonnade). They broke bread in their homes and ate together with glad and sincere hearts, praising God and*

enjoying the favor of all the people. And the Lord added to their number daily those who were being saved (Acts 2:46-47).

Solomon's Colonnade—the idea began to haunt me at least a decade before as our Bible study group was going through the Book of Acts. It was the place in the center of Jerusalem where the early Christians met to publicly worship God and it seemed to be a key dynamic for that fledgling fellowship.

What would it be like for the Church in my nation to daily see the salvation of its fellow citizens? What would a modern-day Solomon's Colonnade look like? While considering these questions, cynicism set in. *What's the point?* I thought, *Isn't our personal salvation and the worship of God in our own fellowship the most important thing?* Why rock the boat? But that day, in the Plaza of Nations, my frozen outlook thawed. As we concluded an exhilarating day united in music and celebration in the center of our city, I was struck with a thrilling burst of vision—the Church of Canada meeting on the streets. My heart declared the impossible: "Here you are, Solomon's Colonnade"!

There was something about the daily-ness of the people of God eating together, worshiping publicly, enjoying the favor of each other that seems to have been a critical element in God's plan to add to the number of the early church. Regrettably, I have observed with great despair how the Church of Canada's membership has been on a drastic and slippery decline. Over the past 40 years, the population of the nation has been radically increasing, but the church population has radically shrinking.

Canadian author Peter C. Newman explains his take on the dilemma in his book, *The Canadian Revolution: From Deference to Defiance*:

> Of all the many institutional touchstones abandoned by Canadians during the past decade, no loss was more wrenching or more personal than the melting away of mainstream churched as a primary source of comfort and exultation.

This was not merely a loss of faith in God, as expressed by declining attendance in places of worship, but a retreat from the Holy Spirit, as expressed by plummeting standards of personal integrity and a pronounced drop in the morality of the churches themselves.[1]

An accurate observation? A rebuke? Have we gone through the motions of presumed spiritual health and seeming righteous practice? Would it be possible for us to find that dynamic sense again of enjoying fellowship with one another with glad and sincere hearts? Is it feasible that we could again be as bold as to display our lives publicly without fear? Could we trust that God himself, not our good church growth plans or effective programs, would add to our number?

Painting the Picture

The swirl of these questions had been circling in our minds for years, but the answers always appeared to exist out of the realm of the viable. As a people and a Church we are too set in our ways; we allow our differences to keep us at a distance from each other; our careless exclusion of and our frivolous presumption with the Holy Spirit are too deeply entrenched.

But something shifted on the day that we dared to "think differently."

After returning from a stint in short term missions, my husband, Russ, and I received a call from an acquaintance, Justyn Rees. We knew Justyn because he frequently spoke at a camp where we served as directors. We loved his Bible story-telling style that was full of captivating British humor. Why he called us on this particular day, he still doesn't know. He didn't need us for anything and we didn't need him since our camp career was finished. He had nothing special to tell us except to ask, "So what are you two thinking of doing next?" His impulsive call and subsequent visit turned out to be providential.

As Justyn sat with us, he casually talked about ideas and thoughts on ministry, we shared experiences from previous years, we conversed about our growing families—all interesting, but not particularly inspiring, until Russ shared, "You know, I've been dreaming of a team of artists, musicians, and actors going out into the streets of the nation to bring a new and unique expression of the love of God."

Justyn leapt into discourse as something ignited his thoughts, "Interesting. For 10 years I've been envisioning how to build a mobile theatre that could be set up in the center of any given town. I'd originally thought that it would be comprised of four double-decker buses…the vision was first sparked in England. But since there aren't many of those in Canada, I've adjusted it to four semi-trailers."

I said nothing—and stared uncomfortably at my reflection in the glass tabletop. Though Russ had mentioned his idea to me before, I wasn't yet onboard with the whole concept. Whenever he mentioned the notion previously I pictured my childhood recollection of the Grimm's fairy tale "The Bremen Town Musicians"—that traveling band of animal minstrels. Perhaps in my imagination, if I went along with the idea, I'd end up being the donkey. And Justyn's plan, well that seemed a little far fetched—four big trucks? What about the expense of all that gas? Where would we get supporters to fund a collection of highway trucks?

At that point I didn't realize that the two visions Russ and Justyn had were very akin to my idea of Solomon's Colonnade—open air, public celebrations. Perhaps I was too afraid of what God was going to ask of me; perhaps I didn't dare believe that God would do with us what He did with the early church. A deep, thoughtful "Hmmm" paused in our minds and on our lips for a moment and the only thing that registered in our thoughts was a united, "Hey, maybe these visions all fit together."

We said our good-byes with no further conclusions, yet over the next three months, there was one fact we could not ignore. As if by divine appointment, at every engagement where we performed, Justyn was the speaker.

There's something about the obvious that prohibits avoidance. Although we weren't yet prepared to succumb to the ambitious idea of the mobile theatre, it was apparent that logically we should at least begin to work together, which we did. The "on the street" concept prompted more questions than we had answers. Who would go? How would we go? What would we do? For me, it all seemed too overwhelming—in my spirit it seemed right, but my mind still couldn't comprehend it. Regardless, in the year ahead God painted a clear picture of His vision at every opportunity.

Confirming the Vision

After a full year of working on small evangelistic initiatives with Justyn, his wife Joy, and their organization, Upstream, the vision seemed to strengthen in all our hearts. It was 1995 and the February chill of Saskatoon, Saskatchewan played host to a conference focused on proclaiming the Gospel to as many Canadians as possible by the year 2000. It challenged us; we had to get out there with our vision. Together we prayed that if it truly was God's desire and if the timing was now, would He please go ahead of us.

We brought the idea before the Upstream board, fully anticipating their response to be: "Are you crazy? Really, four semi-trailers and a mobile team on Canadian streets?! Why don't you do something more tangible, more practical?"

Instead, God spoke His heart through them, "Put out into deep water and let down the nets for a catch," (see Luke 5:4) they said, affirming their overwhelming support for our plan. "We believe that you are to go ahead with this thing right away!" The vision was starting to roll.

Moving On

This book is the expression of a fascinating journey, over five challenging years, of a small team of comfortable Christians who took to the streets of their nation in the spirit of the church's early missionaries. OK, so translate it into the late 1990s version with motorhomes and computers, and cell phones, but the learned principles and the impact of God's leading were certainly as profound for this odd collection of late 20th century believers, as it was for their earlier counterparts. Living full time in trailers, motorhomes, camper vans and host homes, these vagabonds, ranging in age from 0 to 50, set out to traverse the country from Vancouver Island to St. John's, Newfoundland, in an effort to express the love of God to their fellow Canadians.

I was one very challenged mother of two, following along behind this crowd and her visionary husband, in the same way all wives of visionary husbands do, with furrowed brow and clenched teeth saying, "Are you sure about this?" My adventures along the way were going to stretch my character and drastically impact my relationship with my God.

Our main mandate was to encourage the people of our nation to be reconciled to God and to one another, so our marquee became, "For Love of God and Neighbor." We also maintained that the Kingdom of God should be like a party that spills onto the streets and pulls people along as they get caught up in the festivities—our production would be a powerful celebration of God's love and goodness. All these dynamics I whole-heartedly embraced and loved. But reluctance lingered and I wondered, *How do I go to my nation's streets to publicly declare the Gospel?* Well, that was a whole other frightening reality.

Ultimately, the idealistic vision and the reality of the experience proved to be worlds apart. We envisioned ourselves contributing to the moral and spiritual fabric of our nation in historically significant ways through throngs of people responding to our compelling message and noble efforts. The reality was far more humbling—an intensive education in the school of "The Ways of God." (You know, the ones that are higher than ours. As many times as I hear that, I never quite get it.)

With the approach of the year 2000, we echoed the emphasis of many around the world—we wanted to do something for the sake of the new millennium; so we committed to a full time, on-the-road project from 1995 until 2000. In order to traverse our large nation, we needed the time. The long distance we planned to cover did not allow any sort of home base, so we committed ourselves to leaving homes and jobs, friends and family in order to fully accomplish the demands of the endeavor. This, too, had me shaking in my boots.

Going To the Nation

I come from a healthy lineage of skeptical Canadians who truly believe, either from a sense of superior evolution or from a simple lack of evidence, that the amazing things done and seen in the Bible could never happen in our nation here and now. Understandable then, when Russ and Justyn said in May 1995 that they wanted to have the mobile theatre up and running by July 1, I spewed volumes of doubt. Even on the first day of July when I stood before the completed project, I spouted disbelief.

Why is it, while on short- term missions in Asia, I could believe for the world, but here at home I couldn't believe for one bolt. Could it be that my faltering had everything to do with my fear of facing the nation that I love, risking being rejected, or of failing in front of those who know me? I suppose so. I could've escaped the trip by saying I was just not called to do that kind of thing. But my husband was quite certain he had been called, and so he pulled me right along.

As thankful as I am that he did, I respond to the question, "Would you ever do something like that again?" the same way I do after giving birth to children. "Give it to me without the pain and I would do it every day." Our on-the-street project was full of the "gift of adversity"— some physical, some relational, some spiritual—yet it was underscored by the joy of watching God work His miracles in even the most hopeless circumstances. I've concluded that it is all part of the glorious process of being laid out before a Holy God to let Him give birth to His character in and through us—to grow us; to teach us; to see our lives lived out in the fullness of all that He has created us to be; to get us to lay down our rights so that His Kingdom comes and His will is done.

What follows is the account of our supernatural adventure with the Living Jesus—it is the testimony of the principles God was painstakingly bent on showing us, so that His glory would be poured out in our nation, any nation. This was a God-journey that proved to be more life-transforming than we could have conceived, more profoundly wondrous than we imagined, more foundation-shaking than we dared to desire. I write this to encourage my fellow skeptics and to call out our complacent selves into the radical place where the Lord wants His Church to dwell—to the streets of the world where the hungry, thirsty, broken, and lost exist. For the sake of His glory, for the sake of His name.

ENDNOTE

1. Peter C. Newman, *The Canadian Revolution: From Deference to Defiance,* (Toronto, ON: Penguin Books, Canada Ltd., 1995), 23.

CHAPTER 2

Girding the Vision With Prayer

The damp air of the Canadian west coast was the context of our early dreaming. The mountains, rivers, and ocean that surround our beautiful little historic village of Fort Langley, British Columbia, posed the challenge: "Will you relinquish the beauty and comfort of this home in order to pursue…" what?… Obedience. "Go!" is what Jesus said. It was our love for God that pushed us out, yet our love for what God had already blessed us with—our house, community, friends, life of peace and relative ease—presented a potent resistance.

It was May 1995 when we began to share the idea with friends, 20 of whom decided to meet weekly to pray for the items we needed before July 1. Every Wednesday evening we circled together in the music room of our home, sharing and praying for the germinating vision. It was a powerful time—individuals of all denominations came together as the idea ignited in hearts. It was a critical time—a period to seek God, petition for the specifics, refine the vision, fit more pieces of the puzzle. For all of us, this was the first time we saw God answer prayers in such miraculous and pointed ways.

The Prayer

Presumably, the vision is the "what," but prayer is the "how." "How" is where I usually get stuck. My husband, in all his natural innovation ways, provokes a flurry of all of the "what(s)" that need to take place, but my practical little mind is tormented trying to wrap around "how" it might be possible. If I can't figure it out, then I am inclined to conclude that it can't be done. "To prayer, Sandy, to prayer." Prayer places before me new realities and possibilities; causes me to hope for things that my mind could never imagine; allows me to rest in a God who is infinitely more creative and resourceful than I will ever know.

> *And all things you ask in prayer, believing, you shall receive* (Matthew 21:22).

> *No one who puts his hand to the plow and looks back is fit for service in the kingdom of God* (Luke 9:62).

I am thankful that the Lord did not decide whether or not to answer our prayers based on my faith—really I had none. The project was too big, the time frame too tight, the task too imposing, and the cost to my family life too dear. Our only faithfulness was the obedience to go and stand where God had called us to stand, just as He had once commanded the Israelites:

> *You will not have to fight this battle. Take up your positions; stand firm and see the deliverance the Lord will give you...* (2 Chronicles 20:17a).

His faithfulness, as with the Israelites, was evidenced in the fact that the battle, for everything necessary for the project, was accomplished before we arrived—we just needed to go and claim them. Day by day we witnessed the Lord's most astonishing provision.

The Provision

Our initial request was basic. We needed a truck driver, not only to do the obvious, but also to source out the trucks that we would need.

Girding the Vision With Prayer

We met Bob, a smiley, white-haired trucker, a month earlier during an outreach at his church. "What you're gonna need are China-top trailers, but they're hard to find," Bob recommended. "I'll look for what you need," he assured us. Bob was far too busy to join us full-time, but he would help us find trucks. Well, it was a start. In fact, it resulted in more than just a start.

Over the following months, Bob suffered from an illness that lessened his ability to perform his regular work responsibilities. Although he initially helped periodically, after he was miraculously healed while working with us, he was convinced that the Lord was asking Him to continue with us permanently—God's first provision.

During May and June it was rapid-pace answered prayer. We needed money for the "Bandwagon"—$21,000 was provided a week later. Each trailer was going to cost $7,000-$8,000 (we needed four), but Bob miraculously got all four for $11,000. We needed an artist to paint murals on the trailers and discovered Chris, a budding artist who attended the prayer meetings, had said one evening; "All year I've felt God prompting me with scriptures about 'Solomon's Colonnade.' If I'm not mistaken, it seems to me that this project looks like that biblical description."

We prayed for bleachers (six sets to be exact) and just days later Justyn received a random call from a friend who said, "They're tearing down a gymnasium at the school next to us—could you use some bleachers (six sets to be exact)?" On yet another day, Justyn's cell phone rang as he and Russ stood at the lumberyard buying wood to build the stage (the bargain price was also the Lord's intervention), the caller proclaiming, "I've got five carpenters who can come do some building for free if you've got the lumber ready."

The answers to our prayers kept pouring in—volunteers to sand and to paint; a welder to fit the bleachers; an electrician to wire the rigs; a generator; and a sound system. Nothing, except for a baptismal tank, came before we prayed for it and everything arrived right on time, once we did. Amazing!

I've often pondered on the story of Jesus sending His disciples to get the donkey before His entry into Jerusalem (see Luke 19:30). They were to go and untie a donkey, saying to its owner, "The Lord needs it." How did they convince the man to give to a bunch of strangers? Presumably when God goes ahead and we align ourselves with His will through prayer, we intersect with others who have also been listening to Him. In those two months we experienced the same phenomenon. For the most part, the flood of people stepping in to aid us were absolute strangers, each joining in because the vision we shared struck a familiar chord in their hearts—God had already revealed it to them.

Venturing Out

Beyond receiving the practical, material goods, we needed direction. Honestly, who would be willing to work a mission with a group who was saying, "What do we do? Well, we're not really sure, but it has something to do with the Gospel. How long will we stay? Well, until the Lord seems to direct us to move…I guess. How much will it cost? Nothing really, we're trusting God to provide." What a bunch of flakes! But it's how Jesus sent out the 72:

> *After this the Lord appointed seventy-two others and sent them two by two ahead of Him to every town and place where He was about to go* (Luke 10:1).

One of our basic principles was to not lay plans for a mission too far in advance—we wanted to discipline ourselves to go as Jesus' disciples had centuries before us, community to community, step by step, as God led. It seemed important to keep the start and finish of a project somewhat open, in case it was necessary to remain in a town for longer than the allotted time. Additionally, we would only go ahead as God provided. If the finances were not there, we'd stay where we were until God released us by financially verifying the go ahead.

Girding the Vision With Prayer

Again prayer undergirded our every step. Where did we need to go first? Well, Jesus made it clear: *"Jerusalem, Judea and to the outermost parts of the earth...."* Translation: go to your hometown first and expand from there. Believe me, it is nothing short of terrifying to begin in the place where people know you best—friends, neighbors all bearing witness to the stumbling and fumbling of the new initiative. Yet it is what seems to build the credibility and support necessary go ahead and do the same in the next community. We are thankful for a benevolent and compassionate pastor in Justyn's hometown who was willing to take the chance on us as we bungled our way through our first project in Aldergrove, British Columbia.

It was summertime, Canada Day weekend, July 4, 1995, when a handful of us drove ahead to the empty Extra Foods parking lot in the suburban town of Aldergrove. We talked and prayed until suddenly we heard the distinctive rumble of an accelerating transport truck echoing through the barren streets. I cried as others cheered the first of our multicolored trailers into the lot. Phenomenal! God did it!

Fifteen team members joined us full time on this first project. Our efforts in presentation were lacking—a few skits about reconciliation and God; enthusiastic songs with multiple singers and musicians; a short message—meager offerings to a small and unresponsive crowd. What had we gotten ourselves into?

The main signs of life were the hordes of elementary and high school students, freshly released from school to the freedom of summer who wandered through the mall where our Bandwagon was parked. Our interesting venue was a welcome diversion for their already set-in boredom and we immediately took advantage of the opportunity to make friends.

We kept watching for the throngs of people who were supposed to be flocking to our compelling message—they never appeared. Instead, we were abruptly humbled by an average of 50 nominally interested adults, half of whom seemed to have departed by the time our program ended. The students stayed safely around the perimeter of our theatre, preferring to stay aloof from the formal event and chose, rather, to aggravate our attempts to run a smooth and polished program.

Regularly, swarms of neighborhood kids would invade and disrupt the evenings—running or biking through the Bandwagon yelling, grabbing our legs from underneath the trailers as we sang, climbing on the stage to run back and forth during the message. Kids being kids, putting our patience to the test.

Russ creatively devised some rules: Rule #1 No kids on the stage; Rule #2 No kids on the stage; Rule #3 No kids on the stage; Rule #4 There is no rule #4; Rule #5 No kids on the stage. We all echoed the same sentiment and the irritation of having these little critters intruding on our real "adult" ministry. Sadly, we were missing what God was doing.

The youngsters demonstrated their desperate hunger for His truth in the afternoons, when, to our great surprise and delight, they would wander up the bleachers to sit with Leah, and others, who took the time to tell them the story of Jesus. Many of the kids were from broken homes. Most of them had painful stories to tell of the struggles of their lives—all of them were visibly starved for the love and acceptance that we were offering in Jesus' name. Many made a serious commitment to Jesus; none of the adults would. This was going to be one of our journey's most profound lessons.

Location, Location, Location?

Looking in on our work in Aldergrove was a kind, young pastor from nearby White Rock who was actually charged by our vision, not noticing the minimal response we were witnessing on this first project. Here was a man who fully understood that what was happening with the kids was evidence of real fruit and he saw God's fingerprint on our whole endeavor. He promptly invited us to come next to his town and

Girding the Vision With Prayer

immediately set to work gathering organizers, pastors from the ministerial, cooks to provide meals, and sites for our presentation.

Concluding our perplexing three-week project in Aldergrove, we packed up the rigs and made our first vagabond move to the scenic, seaside town of White Rock, British Columbia. It was only a short move but off we went! Unable to secure a single sight for the duration of our stay, frantic organizers arranged for an assortment of non-ideal locales—the isolated back corner of a mall parking lot, the tiny lawn of a beachside Catholic Church, and the grassy lot of an obscure Baptist Church.

It was here our grumbling began, "…this wasn't how it was supposed to be…how was anyone going to find us?…we can't keep setting up and tearing down every week…we want to be in the center of town, not out on the fringes!…what were they thinking?" Sadly, even in our lack of expertise, we were still leaning on our own understanding and trying to accomplish the things of God by the feeble methods of man. Unmistakably, we were relying on the standard North American formula for good marketing: "Location, location, location!"

The early weeks of our White Rock events seemed to confirm our concerns. Anything that we'd learned during our first project seemed to have been shot down in our second. In this upper middle class beach town in the heat of the summer, there were no mall-gathering students; the locals were busy enjoying their vacation on the beach strip 10 blocks from where we were stationed; even the Christians seemed reluctant to attend our presentations. Subsequently our "crowds" were sparse and our attempts to run afternoon kids' programs were embarrassingly futile. Discouragement ruled us.

Our move beachside to the Catholic Church did little to aid in the effort since it was apparently too far from the popular area of beach—there were few passersby, still no crowds. A subtle welling of "why-are-we-doing-this?" regret rose in our throats and a desperate inward conflict ensued as we wrestled to keep our floundering hopes afloat. Persistently, we toddled to our final and most obscure White Rock location on the grassy residential lot of a Baptist Church, pessimistic that our prospects were likely to improve in this least desirable site. But confounding all of our gloomy preconceptions, they came—no rhyme or reason, people just came—and they arrived with an enthusiasm that erupted into impassioned celebration. There in our outdoor theatre, packed to capacity, many publicly and eagerly responded to our message—some even went so far as to be baptized right there in the Bandwagon baptismal tank. The momentum had begun.

For Love of God and Neighbor

We devoted that entire summer and fall to our national project, which we called "For Love of God and Neighbor," finishing projects in Aldergrove, White Rock, Powell River, and Campbell River, British Columbia (our Judea) before the fall winds became frigid and the last of the leaves had fallen. Our homes were our bases, but we stayed in host homes when we ventured to greater distances. Away from home for months on end we lived a strange two-world existence—not part of home, not part of the communities where we ministered. Yes, we began to understand Peter's comment about being, aliens and strangers in the world (see 2 Peter 2:11).

It was a gorgeous summer weather-wise, for which were eternally grateful especially because the Bandwagon had no roof at this point. In fact, for the rainy west coast, it was nothing short of a miracle that we enjoyed three months of glorious sunshine. Only two nights threatened rain. The second project in White Rock had been smothered with summertime sun, but it was early one evening that, for the first time, we prayed desperately for God to hold back the showers that had drenched us throughout that day. In answer to our prayer, at the very moment we began the evening program, the rain ceased and didn't return until the second the program ended. Not surprisingly, just a couple of blocks away, the rain hadn't stopped at all—it was only rainless over the Bandwagon.

During our September event in the next town, Powell River, the rain again let loose and this time it was on the eve of our final night there. Three weeks of astounding crowds and enthusiastic response from this tiny coastal, logging town was thrilling for us, but the pink-tinged sunsets that had scoured the beaches those days of September had finally released their grip to the superior might of a fierce downpour. The hundreds of faithful attendees who huddled in the bleachers were not to be discouraged as they laughed and cheered and celebrated with us in wet sopping clothes and soggy feet. With all that God had done in this town, the rain was a confirmation of the blessing.

Gradually, though, the warmth of summer gave way to the chill of fall, so we borrowed a tent roof from a local camp and carried on. Prayer proved to be our only comfort with the endless rain that plagued a difficult four-week October stay in Campbell River, British Columbia. Like the weather that taunted us, the meager crowds and the general lack of support dampened and chilled our spirits. Taking the liberty to lengthen our stay, first for another week and then for an additional two days, we were determined to linger until there was some sort of breakthrough in this challenging community. "What's going on here Lord?" "Why does there seem to be so much resistance?" "Show us how to reach this place."

And then something we had never experienced before started to happen—God began to reveal the main dilemma of the town through dreams and visions. Specifically, the Church at large had lost its effectiveness due to disunity. We spoke boldly to church leaders, who then met, and repented, en masse and immediately the breakthrough came, both in weather and in community response. As the people of the church were finally convinced of their need to work together, they flooded into the Bandwagon to join with us in proclaiming the love of God to their neighbors. People from all over the community (including students dressed up as ghouls) crowded the Bandwagon, astounded by the power of the celebration. Even the eggs thrown at the Bandwagon went essentially unheeded because people were so caught up in the party.

You Who Go Down to the Sea

As winter weather set in, we stored the Bandwagon and the team made plans to return to our homes. But we dared to pray one last time, "Lord is there somewhere else you want us to go; something else you want us to do before the year is out?" In the back of our minds, most of us were hoping for a "No-it's-ok-you've-already-worked-so-hard" response from the Lord. It didn't come. Instead came the prompting, "Coast to coast…" We still hadn't traveled to the distant and sparsely populated western coast and notably, an invitation had come to us from a pastor there.

So in December 1995, leaving the Bandwagon behind, the team journeyed by ferry to Vancouver Island, drove the winding coastal highway to its end, bumped along logging roads, and finally jumped into private motorboats to reach Kyuquot. On this remote collection of tiny, beautifully wooded islands live the most fascinating assortment of people—fishermen, loggers, hermits, artists—all centered on a native fishing village.

Sleeping on whatever was available (for some of the girls, it was shelves), miserably sick with dysentery, bones chilled from the continuous deluge of rain and blustering wind, the Upstream team took the message to the sea. In the schools, community centers, the church of Kyuquot, and the nearby villages of Tahsis and Zeballos, we shared the Gospel. Activity-starved locals crowded into buildings to catch the skits, music, and message of the Christmas story. Dozens of native children swarmed the venues, adding to the chaotic struggle of our still ripening methods of presentation; but friendships were birthed and the love of God through Jesus was given a home in many hearts. A gruff young man, Derek, was so compelled by the message that after giving his life over to the Lord, in reckless abandon he burned down his disheveled mobile home and jumped on the Bandwagon to join our team as a maintenance man.

Our mission and its calling was taking shape and our band of ambassadors was growing. Prayer, undeniably, had become the iron rails on which our cross-nation venture was being aligned. Bit by bit we were discovering the intricate facets of this faith walk as God methodically unfolded His purposes before us and subversively infiltrated our ranks with His loving character and His flesh-confounding ways.

CHAPTER 3

Going With Nothing

Now it is one thing to get an enormous production like the Bandwagon on the road, but it is a whole other challenge to keep it, and the team to man it, rolling. The only conclusion we came to was the seemingly feeble cliché, "The Lord will provide!" Aha, but don't be fooled, it wasn't feeble at all—it was a strategically critical principle for our weak knees, faint hearts, and desperate need for control. It's an inherited thing.

Like Boy Scouts gone too far, we North Americans have turned the motto "Always Be Prepared" into an 11th Commandment. I cannot tell you the number of times I have heard people say, "God could be asking you or me to do a crazy thing in faith, but He's given us a brain." Always intimating that it is a foolish thing to just step out and do something without having, as my mother would say, "all of your ducks in place." This does not exclude the seasons when we are to plan and prepare—and please note the crazy things are by the call of the Lord, not by our own whims.

Picture us North Americans as Noah's neighbors, "Well hey, buddy, it's not practical to get two of every animal, I mean, God's given you a brain!" Counseling Moses: "Come on, we're not gonna part the Red Sea or anything, God's given us a brain!" As friends of Peter: "Man, what kind of over-developed ego have you got that you'd ask to walk on water—He gave you a brain?"

"The fear of the Lord is the beginning of wisdom; all who follow in His precepts have good understanding" (Ps. 111:10). Get it? Fear of the Lord, not brainpower is the key to making wise decisions. Why? Because many of the things the Lord calls us to do, don't seem wise to our human understanding. This principle may seem simplistic, but for our comfortable Western society, it is a difficult thing to live out.

Like Jesus sending out the 72, another part of the vision was that we were to go without purse or bag or sandals (see Luke 10). We would begin our trek without everything we needed for the trip and trust that God would provide it as we needed it; and, we would go to communities as the Lord directed, not according to their ability to pay for us to come.

I Send You Out

So it was with our first project in Aldergrove—out of our own scanty pockets came all of the printing and advertising costs for the events, and our daily meals, which we shared with the local collection of kids and students who never seemed to have the need to go home. But God's people quickly click into gear when they see a need. One woman, noticing all of the young kids around, took it upon herself to begin an onsite day camp. Others brought food and made meals. One man decided that we needed his help with the sound system and guitar playing. Thierry, a Swiss friend, even flew in from Belgium to be a part of things and to encourage us along. As people began to see the vision in motion they joined in.

As Tamera, one of the team, was walking home one day, she was thinking about the interest and eagerness of all the youth and prayed, "Lord, we've got these kids interested in what we're doing, but we can't get them all to the Bandwagon because of transportation limitations. Please, would you provide a van?" To her great amazement, the moment she stepped into the house that day, there was word that a brand new van had just been donated to Upstream. God is so specific. For Tamera, relationship with those youth opened the way for conversation about God; conversation gave opportunity for response to the love of God; response turned to commitment. As a result, about a dozen kids, ages 10-15, gave their lives to Jesus—some were even baptized. "The Lord will provide." True.

Generosity

What seems to happen when one walks out with nothing is a freedom of generosity. When you have nothing, everything is a gift. Often people are apprehensive to give if uncertain of the need, but when there is nothing, everything they have to give fills a need; the joy of giving is released.

While in Vancouver Island's seaside town of Campbell River (October '95), the "going-with-nothing" team suddenly found themselves without anything to weather the piercing wind and biting cold daily experienced in the frigid, sodden Bandwagon—morale was plummeting. Opposite our site was a line-up of strip mall businesses whose workers and shoppers daily gaped at us as we carried on in the blustery weather. Thankfully the local Work Warehouse owner spotted our need. In compassion, he invited us in to take, at his expense; whatever was necessary to survive the cold—coats, boots, sweaters, hats, socks, and long underwear. And then, just at the moment when we were feeling guilty for accepting so much, the same man arrived with a large bag overflowing with thermal socks, hats, and gloves. An enormous and astounding provision.

Sometimes, too, the provision was even more personal. My eldest daughter, Tadia, and I had to lay before the Lord a simple prayer request: "Please God, Tadia needs sandals, boots, and running shoes for the next season and we have no money to purchase them. Will you provide what she needs?" It wasn't until a couple of months later, after we had completely forgotten about the request, when a bag of clothing landed at our door. Among the pants, sweaters, and shirts were three pairs of shoes—sandals, boots, and runners—all in Tadia's size. The woman who had given them had no idea of our need. Even more miraculously, my fashion-conscious Tadia liked them all!

> *For the pagans run after all these things* (i.e. food, drink, clothing), *and your heavenly Father knows that you need them. But seek first His kingdom and His righteousness and all these things will be given to you as well* (Matthew 6:32-33).

Believing for Homes

God had been building our faith for His provision, but each need brought the same challenge of faith for provision, and skepticism was consistently hard to shake. The next great faith venture was in the form of on-the-road homes. For most and for a limited amount of time, billeting in host homes was manageable, but for us, as time on the road stretched out and personal and family space became critical, more room was needed.

For our family, each day of living in parking lots, with lampposts as our trees and asphalt as our yard, the urgency to improve our daughters' quality of life was growing. "What toilets do we use today mommy?" Kezia, then 4 years old, would say. "Watch out for the cars!" I'd caution constantly. "I'm starving, where can I get food this time?" asked the growing Tadia. Kezia: "Should I go to bed in the van now dad?" We struggled to offer even the basic elements of life for our girls in this strange parking lot existence. We needed to have our own space.

A motorhome was the most logical remedy but a major item like this, and for us, was again beyond my realm of faith. Like an Israelite in the wilderness I began to grumble, especially since we would daily drive past dealership lots full of motorhomes—to remind us to pray perhaps, but at the time, I figured it was to torment us.

I was confronted with the test as we faced the first of our projects away from our home territory. My prayer was in part protest, as I declared too forcefully, "I won't be going unless we have a mobile residence for our family!" It was conceivably the chance for my faithless heart to opt out of the whole crazy notion of traveling the nation and an opportunity to resign to my fears of stepping out. But the bitter response in my heart was an indication of my own stubbornness—I knew God was calling me to give up my home and, frankly, I didn't want to. I couldn't believe that He was going to provide all that my family needed. What's more, I still couldn't trust that He was going to give us success in our work.

But as Barney, the purple dinosaur, once said to one of his skeptics (forgive me, I'm a mother over-educated in children's television), "You may not believe in me, but I still believe in you." God is gracious to work even with our faithlessness—He can't help but be faithful. Early the next morning, Justyn called to say that there was a small trailer waiting for us at our destination in Powell River. Amazingly, that loan was duplicated again in the next town, with a luxurious 37' motorhome; and by the beginning of the next season, one of our supporting families had committed to purchasing for us, a motorhome of our own.

> *Give, and it will be given to you. A good measure, pressed down, shaken together, running over, will be poured into your lap. For with the measure you use, it will be measured to you* (Luke 6:38).

In a Tiny Little Living Space

Now, the provision of billets and trailers was a great blessing, but the natural need for personal space became a whole other frontier of challenge. I recall, in my university psychology studies, an experiment where psychologists methodically decreased the size of living space given to a community of mice—the mice would gradually become more and more agitated and violent, eventually resorting to gnawing on one another. I know the feeling. Call it a survival response, but there is something that rises up in one's previously composed nature when there are people always in your personal space.

Upstream team members Christie and Georgia had to share a room in one host home where, if Christie wanted to get up to go to the toilet in the night, Georgia had to climb out to fold up and move her sofa bed from in front of the door. Justyn and his wife Joy were required to administrate the entire Upstream organization from the trunk of their Honda. In one host home, Trucker Bob was plunked down in middle the children's bedroom and all the children slept in there with him.

The hilarity of these circumstances for some reason didn't have the same humor at the time. The frustration of having to "make do" can impair our thankfulness and can cripple our joy. Ultimately it looks as though God has provided, but not quite adequately. Does He not properly understand our need? Is He not concerned for us? I suppose that is exactly why God allows us these experiences—there is a depth and a breadth of our need that we don't see and He wants us to trust Him and to receive from Him with thankful hearts.

Georgia and Christie's early housing adventures began to produce in them a persistence in prayer, requesting their own small closet (say, a trailer) from which to get time alone, to spend time with Him. Each received a trailer within the year. Justyn and Joy dug into prayer and connected with a ministry in Europe that was closing down operations and had finances to donate to another ministry. The resulting gift provided their first mobile office, a motorhome. And for Bob, the children he bunked with offered the unconditional love and acceptance this lonely middle-aged man needed. Hugs and kisses and tears, his included, were poured out at his departure.

Conclusion: God knows our need. Yes!

Waiting and Giving

Never having known war or want, I see that my indulged, indulgent generation and I *expect* a comfortable way of life. God continually provides for us, but we don't always see because of our hunger for *more* and our pressure to have it *now*! What a discipline it is, then, to learn to really wait for God. He knows what we need and will always provide for us, but He allows hunger in our lives so He can make His love a practical human reality.

God had mercy on us and was teaching us to pray simply, *"Give us today our daily bread...."* (Matt. 6:11) so that we could readily see His provision and recognize our abundance. With an entire team going with nothing, it is amazing how we become so easily aware of one another's needs. My extra ten dollars may be the provision that my fellow worker has been waiting for. When everyone has little, it doesn't take much to feel rich and to feel the freedom to share the wealth.

I had been praying in private desperation for a couple of months that God would provide dental work for our daughters. As a matter of fact, I was so afraid of how much it was going to cost, I couldn't even bring myself to make appointments, though I knew Tadia's teeth needed immediate work. Late one evening, Georgia apprehensively approached me, and placing a check in my palms, she declared, "I have here $200 for your family and, this is going to sound weird, but I think it's to be spent on the dentist." I started to weep. How could she have known? I had told no one.

Seeing my obvious emotion, she said, "You see, last week I got some financial support from friends, but there was $200 more than what I needed. I began to pray for God to let me know where I should give the extra money. Last night I woke up in middle of the night and saw a picture of you, Sandy, but when you smiled your normally beautiful smile at me, you exposed a mouth full of completely rotten teeth. I concluded that God wanted me to give you money for the dentist."

Manna

In our day of securities—retirement funds, life insurance, savings accounts, unemployment insurance, educational funds—it is a challenge not to miss the opportunities that God gives us to learn to let Him provide. He speaks it to our spirits, not to our heads. It is an opportunity to resist the fear of being without, and to not allow fear to contaminate our faith in His abundance.

But then comes along the "Manna Principle." God promises first and foremost to provide for our needs, but He requires us to understand the difference between our *needs* and our *wants*. Sometimes He feeds us, as He did the Israelites, with manna—basic, daily provision—so we learn to be thankful and trusting.

As our national mission wore on, we became more organized and managed to encourage our host communities to cater our dinner meals—manna! What a treat after trying to barbecue for 15+ people outside everyday in the Bandwagon. With all of the creativity that overflows from Canadian kitchens, it's surprising that any of our catered meals would be duplicated. But when taco salad was served to us five dinners in a row (all different towns) and lasagna seven times in a row (different churches in another town), we had to take notice. It was on the occasion we were eating chili for two weeks that the team really began to grumble. To strengthen the point, on our family's day off, a friend who lived nearby was going to treat us to a home-cooked meal, to which we breathed a sigh of relief. What did she serve? Chili! She said it was the first time she'd served it in years.

The same test to the Israelites in the wilderness was ours: when the manna gets monotonous, will we grumble, or will we give thanks? Fortunately, the great blessing of the Lord's tests are that we never fail, He just says, "Take another lap"—40 years of laps for the Israelites;

lasagna and chili laps for the Upstream team. He wants us to look completely to Him, not to what He is providing. Our grumbling is symptomatic of unbelief and unthankfulness.

Is it any wonder that after weeks of manna, the Israelites were saying, "Where's the meat?" God hadn't forgotten them, but He knew what they were starting to acknowledge as being more important than Him—their stomachs! Looking at how our project began, the provision of any food was a big blessing, but how quickly we forget and our greedy little selves hunger for bigger and better.

With the Israelites, God responds to their complaining by sending quail, but have you ever caught on that it's not a good thing (see Exodus 16)? As a matter of fact, He claims that there would be so much, it would come out of their noses. In the same way, following our complaints about chili, God sent a massive roll of turkey loaf, on which Upstream joyfully feasted during a lavish meal that we pridefully made (i.e. "We'll make for ourselves the kind of meal we really want!"). But there was so much, and our portions were so large, we began to feel sick. When another roll of the same turkey loaf was donated the following week, we all groaned, comprehending the "quail out of their noses" phenomenon—we couldn't eat another bite.

Potato salad meals for six weeks solid was how the Lord got rid of our lasagna-griping. Meal after meal, as we arrived for dinner time, God challenged us to be thankful for yet another variation of the spud/mayonnaise concoction. And we passed the test, even as an ice cream scooped dollop of bright Big Bird yellow and another of bright Barney purple, both apparently birthed from the same potato/egg genealogy, sat lumped on our plates, confronting our internal fortitude. Smiling at one another for God's little reminder to us, we thanked God everyday for His generous provision, and on the day lasagna was served, we all cheered!

(So not mislead you, we have conversely experienced a plethora of great meals—turkey, ham, roast beef, moose, lobster, and cabbage rolls—as a testimony to a God who lavishes good things on His children.)

To pray with expectancy causes us to believe in our good and loving God and His good and loving gifts, even when the current circumstances don't seem to confirm it. The time of waiting seems bent on stirring in us, an urgency to dig into God—to keep looking to Him for His provision; to thank Him for His answer; to remember that He is good all the time; to let go of any selfish inclinations connected to our requests; to understand another part of His character that we've not seen before.

CHAPTER 4

Standing Between God and Man— Worship, Evangelism, and Intercession

Taking more time than anticipated, we finally started to get a feel for what God had purposed for us on this uncommon trek across the nation and, I'll pause here for a moment to give you a taste of what we did:

1. Evangelism—Not the stereotypical TV evangelists, but simply anyone who would stand before the people, on behalf of God, and plead for them to return to Him.

2. Intercession—Standing before God in prayer, on behalf of the people, to plead with Him to have mercy.

3. Worship—Leading the celebration of the relationship between God and man.

On any programmed evening the theatre burst with music and dance as we introduced the people of the community to the Lord of the party—Jesus. Children crowded the stage, people from every walk of life joined hands to dance in circles, or two-by-two linking elbows to spin each other. Into the middle of the party came clowns, who mimed a message of reconciliation, or comical actors presented a play addressing key salvation issues. And finally it was all woven together by the testimony of one of our team and with a speaker bringing the message of salvation through Jesus Christ.

Making the Introduction

During the day we would visit neighborhoods with local Christians inviting people to the Bandwagon in the evening, or pray with them. Some schools, seniors' homes, detention centers, psychiatric hospitals, youth drop-in centers would open their doors and allow the musicians and clowns to bring the message of hope right into their facilities. One by one Canadians were being touched by God's heart for our nation to return to Him.

This first part of our mandate, evangelism, was the toughest to begin to do. We Canadians don't enter this arena too boldly. Where the Americans have thousands of evangelists, Canadians have only a handful. Why? It's likely because of our high regard for political correctness—our sincere fear of offending others. Regrettably, we have stepped away from the wonderful gift of introducing our friends and neighbors to Jesus. (For an inspiring handbook about this topic, read Justyn Rees' *Love Your Neighbor For God's Sake*[1].)

How did we go about it? Initially we sent an artistic Upstream postcard to every home—a compelling invitation to the Bandwagon complete with a brief explanation of our message. Then we would approach people personally: knocking on doors, one-on-one relationships, connecting with people on the street. And finally we presented the Gospel in a larger public setting: short plays, story-telling, songs, and a message— in the Bandwagon or wherever we were invited.

Of course personal connections were the best, but on one occasion, it was the impact of our invitation that opened the way. This particular Wednesday, Matthew picked up his mail off the floor and began to shuffle through the junk pieces that were littered among the important letters. He spotted our brightly colored postcard and pulled it free from the bundle. "What is this?"

"It's an appeal to God to heal our division and an appeal to each other to be reconciled. Love, not legislation will unite us, and love starts in the heart of each Canadian."

"Yeah," he thought, *"That's how it should be. I agree that it's God who will make a difference in all our lives."* Overwhelmed by this truth, he felt suddenly gripped by an urgency to declare something he had never even thought of before—an unseen force was prompting him to say, "I confess that Jesus Christ is Lord!" The whole episode both thrilled and frightened him to such a degree that he waited a full week before he dared to enter the doors of the Bandwagon. After he arrived, he was so convinced of the truth of the Gospel; he immediately wanted to be baptized. His mother, similarly compelled by his testimony, did the same a few days later.

We've been learning to do the work of evangelism, giving account for the hope that is within us, in any circumstance—this is a mandate to all of the church. The job of the evangelist is to *equip* the church to do evangelism, not to stand in lieu of the church to do it. One of the Upstream team discovered this fact as he was driving one day and picked up a hitchhiker who declared, "I'm on a journey to find myself." Well, the journey took just six hours because throughout the trip our Upstreamer shared his testimony. By the time they reached their destination, the man had resolved that he found his identity, it was in Jesus.

Evangelism? It is simply a matter of beginning an introduction to the Creator of the universe; it is a compelling testimony of His real impact in real lives; it is practical expressions of an unconditional love and acceptance; it is an urging of a neighbor to reconcile their relationship with their Heavenly Father; it is a love that cares enough to look behind a closed door to minister to a broken heart.

Standing in the Gap

Our second mandate, intercession, is one of those mysterious disciplines seemingly reserved for those who have the stamina to spend long hours in somber, pensive meditation, and prayer. We were initially looking for those "types" to fill this role but we quickly discovered that prayer warriors are a rare and elusive breed and it became increasingly apparent that God wanted, no *needed*, more. He wanted to recruit each of us—ADD (Attention Deficit Disorder) types included. We began to understand that true intercession is simply a state of desperation; it is being moved by God's heart of love for the people of the nation; it is knowing that we deserve judgment, but then pleading with the Lord to relent in sending His wrath.

A group of praying people in one struggling town taught us best. This conglomeration of everyday citizens—homemakers, business people, professionals, retirees, and pastors—were from different churches in the community, who, out of that sense of fierce desperation, managed to find one another and meet each week to pour their hearts out to the Almighty. "God, we pray for the youth—that they would find hope." "We ask that you would turn us from worshiping gods other than you." "Jesus, please strengthen your Church." "Lord please heal this marriage…that illness…these hearts." Nothing complicated or contrived, just simple and honest dialogue with the God who loves them, and they were observing daily answers to their prayers.

Similarly, as we traveled town to town, our key objective was to find the places in a town where, by disobedience to God, the walls of righteousness had been broken down—street by street, house by house and person by person, from hilltops, around churches, in historical places, at government buildings—we stood there in prayer to plead for God's mercy and for Him to invade each place. As someone once proclaimed, "Peace is not the absence of war, it is the presence of God." Further, we made public effort in our Bandwagon events to rebuild those walls by calling the people to turn from their disobedience.

Admittedly this was not an easily palatable, or politically correct, thing to do in Canada, but it was impossible to ignore that it was absolutely critical.

The mystery of intercession is about allowing God to break our hearts with the things that break His heart so that we will stand in the gap between His judgment and the sin of the people—it is the act of running to the refuge of the Lord to claim "sanctuary" within the walls of His mercy. As God Himself has declared:

> *I looked for a man among them who would build up the wall and stand before me on behalf of the land so I would not have to destroy it, but I found none* (Ezekiel 22:30).

Like Moses, standing before the Lord to entreat Him to stop the advancing plague of His anger for their rebellion (see Numbers 14) and saying, "Over my dead body will you bring judgment on these people." Like David running out beyond Jerusalem to face the Lord's killing angel (see 2 Samuel 24:17), saying, "Over my dead body will you bring judgment on these people." Like Daniel fasting in sackcloth and ashes imploring the Lord to not bring His desolation of Jerusalem (see Daniel 9) saying, "Over my dead body will you bring judgment on these people." Like Jesus, innocent and hanging on a cross saying, "Over my dead body will you bring judgment on these people." This place in the gap is where we join Jesus to plead for love of God and neighbor.

In Spirit and Truth

"If music be the food of love, play on."[2] If God is love, perhaps music is the means to give people a taste of relationship with divine true love. Play on. Love songs to and from God can foster an honest hunger for the Lord himself. This was our third mandate, worship.

Russ and I had already spent a number of our earlier years writing and singing worship tunes for a student discipleship ministry we had pioneered in our city and we knew how effectively music could draw the hearts of a generation—power and hope were released and lives were gripped by words expressing real, life-transforming Truth. Here in the Bandwagon all generations were joining in to proclaim the love of God with worship, and we were quickly observing its effectiveness on the streets.

On one particular day, Don, from White Rock, could hear the pleasant strains of music as he hoisted his groceries into the trunk of his car. Curiosity taunted his interest and enticed him to discover the source of the sound. There in the rear of Semiahmoo Mall parking lot, he spotted our strangely painted rigs. "Wow, what is this?" he asked Russ. "It's a celebration of the love of God," Russ said. Don couldn't resist—he sat down in the stands, riveted by the intriguing message through music.

On another day, the Marchand family was taking a quiet evening stroll down their neighborhood street and heard music wafting through the grove of trees. Finding a tiny footpath through the woods, father led the foursome to the music's extraordinary source—to the local high school parking lot, which was oddly inhabited by a curious collection of bizarre vehicles. "We could hear the wonderful sound of your music through the trees," he said to the greeter at the door. Smiling at their astonishing find, the four climbed up into the bleachers to enjoy the entire program.

Worship is the wind that fans into flame embers of faith—putting words of praise onto the lips of agnostics and surprising the atheist with the convincing reality of God's presence. Most of the music we used we wrote ourselves, that way the church people were on the same ground as those outside the church; everyone was learning together. Besides, Scripture tells us again and again to "Sing to the Lord a new song" (see Psalm 149:1a). We are told to put our worship into our own words. Our style? A little bit of everything—eclectic like the nation. Catchy and compelling, with plenty of drums and fiddle and guitar to suit all generations and cross cultural barriers.

On Stringed Instruments

Just a note about the fiddle/violin. If you haven't noticed, this ancient instrument is rarely seen in the church setting these days—yet it is one of the most visibly prominent musical influences in our culture, from symphonies to folk to rock music, even hip hop artists are using it these days. Why? In a historical commentary on church music, author Ray Hughes gives an enlightening explanation of its demise in North America. He observes that, "…for many years the church imposed the belief that the fiddle was the devil's box."[3] Ray's research has discovered that an entire Irish population of early North American settlers were forced to abandon this, their cultural music, because the church of the day rejected it—the impact has remained for generations.

Kathleen, a talented violin player, had ministered with us for several years and was now part of the Upstream team. In our limited creative scope, the violin seemed useful for little besides the odd foot-stomping tune or a soothing mellow ballad—musical preference highlighted the electric guitar as the solo instrument. By providence or by simple expiration, our guitar players seemed to consistently dissolve from our ranks, leaving us in a constant artistic lurch, and by default, we began to focus on the violin, writing songs with a uniquely Canadiana Celtic flavor.

We were thrilled to discover that, unbeknownst to us, the fiddle (what you *must* call it in certain regions) added an energetic and accessible musical style that was relevant to Canadian culture from west to east. Additionally, in our desire to see worship involve the heart, soul, mind, and strength, we discovered that fiddle music naturally and painlessly gets "comfortable" people of all generations and ethnicities rejoicing, clapping, and out-of-their-seats dancing in a non-threatening manner.

Doing Battle

Musically, our motive was to keep producing "cool" music that appealed to our finicky contemporaries, yet still express the powerful truths we believed. But what we had not anticipated was that it would also be a potent tool of warfare. When we lift the name of Jesus (more in Chapter 6), proclaim the promises of God and His character, there is work done in the heavenlies for the sake of God's glory. Someone once explained to us that if satan is the "prince of the powers of the air" (see Ephesians 2:2) then anything that makes sound waves, especially in worship to Jesus, disturbs satan's domain. If that is true, then the more the music, the more sound, the more battle done!

In White Rock that first summer, there seemed to be an amount of resistance to our presence. To the small number at the mall and the beachside Catholic Church we kept on with our music and message, praising Jesus to only a few humans, yet presumably to many in the heavenly realm. It wasn't until we proceeded to the obscure location of the Baptist church in our third week, that our praises broke through—crowds of people filled the Bandwagon and an enthusiastic response to our message ensued. It was a phenomenon we discovered worked consistently to shake off spiritual heaviness in a place. We would stay late after the commencement of a program and worship, lifting up a canopy of praise where the Spirit of God could dwell—the days that followed always seemed significantly more fruitful.

With all our Might

We would dance too, just spontaneous celebration because of the sheer joy of God's love. It's the same picture from Graham Kendrick's song, "The Lord is Marching Out in Splendor":

> His army marches out with dancing
> For He has filled our hearts with joy
> Be glad the kingdom is advancing
> The love of God our battle cry.

Music that is celebrative and enthusiastic draws people, and the truth of Scripture in song has the ability to pour the knowledge of God right through the mind and directly into the appetite of a hungry heart. Hosea 4 expresses that the corruption and immorality in the land was caused by the "lack of the knowledge" of God—the restoration of truth is what our generation is hungry for and expressing it through music becomes revolutionary and transforming!

A man stood quietly at the back of the auditorium one evening as we finished our music and Justyn had just begun to speak. As I ambled toward the man, he whispered enthusiastically, "Great message!" "Yeah, Justyn has a great gift for communicating," I said. "Oh yeah, he's good too, but I meant the music."

For one who rarely pays attention to the actual words to songs (for the longest time, I thought that "And can it be that I should gain…" was a song about weight), I have been learning what some already know—music can radically impact the heart and precipitate transformation in the inner person. It was a young musician who King Saul called on when his inner life was in turmoil. He witnessed the soothing impact of the presence of God and freedom from debilitating spiritual powers, through the David's worship of His Lord God.

Love in the Family of God

Further, our unified worship is the demonstration of the impact of His love. Corporate worship is the introduction of the Bride herself, and though some are in the habit of presenting Jesus while intentionally side-stepping the Church, we truthfully can't go out to introduce the Groom (Jesus) without also introducing the Bride (the Church). It is one of the most profound proclamations of our unity (or lack thereof).

In that first year of our endeavor, we were grasping the gravity of this concept. We noticed interested looks across the Bandwagon floor as people spotted work mates that they didn't know were Christians; former church members who joined other churches or been part of church splits; people of adversarial denominations supporting the same message. And then as they all stood together to worship the same

Jesus, the lines of division disappeared. All are children of the Father—one Church—one Bride.

We have discovered this to be a wonderful challenge to the Church—if we are expressing to our communities who we are—the very Body of Christ—we can't hide the cracks, the divisions, and the politeness that masks our lack of intimacy with one another and with God. Truly, we are forced to deal with the things that divide us and to learn how to honestly love one another. Humble repentance and unified worship are the hallmarks of a welcoming Church ready for revival.

ENDNOTES

1. Justyn Rees, *Love Your Neighbor For God's Sake.* (London, UK: Hodder and Stoughton Ltd., 1997).
2. William Shakespeare, *Twelfth Night.*
3. Ray Hughes, *Sound of Heaven, Symphony of Earth.* (Fort Mill, SC: MorningStarPublications, 2003).

Chapter 5

Waiting for God

The vision of our on-the-street mission, prompted and established in obvious ways by God, had the frustrating inclination to get hidden in the cloud of our expectation and impatience. Within the first year, we were struggling to hold fast to this strange way of walking—by faith, by the Word of the Lord, step by step, not laying plans too far ahead, etc. At times an unexpected wave of events would tip us off balance, knock us to our knees and though we'd keep trying our darnedest to get back up, on our knees was where God wanted us to be. It's how we hear Him best.

A Change in Season

Leaving the Bandwagon behind for the winter, we built bunks into a highway bus and set off as a pack of wide-eyed pioneers heading east—doing indoor outreaches (is that an oxymoron?) as an opportunity to scope out the land where we would eventually settle our rigs.

We were still determined to go into the towns where Jesus led us, but really, the freezing temperatures of Edmonton, Alberta, in the dead of winter? We weren't wise enough to know that it's not brave to sleep in a bus as the thermometer plunges to arctic-cold temperatures, it's just stupid. We battled to stay ahead of hypothermia and struggled to keep body parts and sleeping bags from freezing to bus walls. Every evening I'd bundle 5-year-old Kezia into leggings and a thermal undershirt, pajamas, sweater, socks, hat, and mitts, and then firmly tucked her under layers of blankets, praying desperately that she wouldn't wiggle out from under them in the night.

Laughter is the water and prayer the pill to relax the stress and keep spirits light in the turmoil of absurd, adverse circumstance. When "Gus," our bus, wouldn't start after a night in the frigid cold of Jasper National Park, we crowded together in the men's bathroom—singing, joking, and even holding a Bible study—in a valiant effort to warm our numbed body parts. We skied and skated the barren and icy farming roads of Manitoba as we waited for a tractor to pull Gus out of a snow-blown ditch. We found refuge from the blizzarding snow in the dorms of Providence Bible College when Gus slid into another ditch.

A storage bay in Trinity Television Studios housed our mobile hotel in the wintry freeze of Winnipeg. While there we had not adequately anticipated the consequences of team member Mark's well-known nighttime wanderings. It was the silent hour of 2 A.M. and Mark was suddenly in need of a bathroom facility. Stumbling out of the bus, he opened the door to the building and bam! The security alarms went off. Chaos ensued as Mark frantically scrambled to find Russ for the alarm shut-off code. Alarm assaulting, Russ couldn't find the paper with the code on it. In the meantime, Kathleen, on a nocturnal quest for Tylenol to ease her splitting headache, had no relief; and Chris was pacing the aisle amidst the anarchy with hand to head repeating, "Tylenol? Tylenol!"

And to intensify the whole experience I was now under the nauseous fog of my recently confirmed pregnancy. Oh yes, just to heighten the thrill of our travel adventure, I was now two months pregnant and due to deliver in July 1996. What was God thinking? Didn't He know what we had just committed to? How was I going to deal with a baby on the road? "To prayer, Sandy, to prayer."

"No one who puts his hand to the plow and looks back…" Yeah, yeah, yeah…

Shortsightedness and Waiting

As the spring of our second year (1996) arrived, the perceived pressure to come up with a plan before our Upstream team members threatened to scatter caused us to accept an invitation to go to Sault St. Marie (pronounced "Soo Saint Marie") to participate in an evangelism conference. Not a bad choice except that it was halfway across the country (a four-day journey away) and it wasn't quite what we felt we were to be doing as a team. But we had to have something planned, and surely God would provide for us as He always had.

So in April 1996, after completing two brief projects with the revived Bandwagon in Fort Langley and Langley, our 15-member team had packed up all of their possessions and rendezvoused at the Rees home in preparation to leave for Sault St. Marie. For Russ and I, it was the final letting go of our beloved Fort Langley home. We wept as we sold our furniture, stuffed the remaining items in a storage unit and dubiously drove away in our new abode—a 24' motorhome.

As a team, we had conveniently ignored the "step by step" principle, but God was going to catch us on the "as the Lord provides" principle. The day that we entered the Rees house, the Lord shut the door—the finances for Upstream remained outside a closed door—literally not a penny came to us for 40 days and 40 nights.

We didn't see it coming. For the first 48 hours, we remained hopeful, "God will provide at the last minute like we've seen Him do before." We prayed, enjoyed each other's company, and kept looking to the horizon for the approaching provision. By the close of 10 days, everything began to unravel. "Where is God?" "Has He forgotten us?" "But we just left everything!" "Whose fault is it?"

Listening

The middle 20 days of the 40 were a painful time of growth. Our peaceful and loving relationships suddenly witnessed their first depth test—tempers flared; individuals threatened to leave; animosity grew; criticism flourished; the guys' inconsiderate volume of food consumption became a cause to declare war.

We spent our entire time doing the most agonizing thing that our busy little selves could possibly imagine—nothing! We had to cancel our involvement in the Sault St. Marie event—any other opportunities we tried to initiate wouldn't take root. It was an excruciating period of getting ourselves to pause long enough to listen to God. Daily we studied from the Book of Genesis, where each passage was screaming out our lesson: *"Not by the arm of the flesh, but by the hand of the Lord! Not by the arm of the flesh, but by the hand of the Lord!"*

Adam and Eve eating the forbidden fruit (Ch. 1); Abraham begetting Ishmael (Ch. 16); Isaac lying to Abimelech about his wife (Ch. 26); Jacob deceiving Isaac for the blessing (Ch. 27); Joseph boasting of his vision of greatness to his brothers (Ch. 37). All were attempts to bring about the events that the Lord was already promising would occur— eternal life with God (Adam); a son (Abraham); safety and prosperity (Isaac); God's blessing (Jacob); leadership and authority (Joseph)—but not waiting for Him to accomplish it. God seemed to be assuring us, as He did Abraham, *"I [am] your very great reward"* (Genesis 15:1). It would not be what we accomplished that would give us success; it would be God's very presence with us that would be the prize. This cloak of humility was drawing us to say, like Moses, *"If your Presence does not go with us, do not send us up from here"* (Exodus 33:15).

And so we waited…and waited…and waited. By the final 10 days of the 40, we'd been transformed. Anxiety and fear had been replaced by the peace, hope, and joy resident in our place of rest with God. He would be faithful to see us through what He was calling us to do. The day after the 40th day, a small miracle surfaced—a Bandwagon project commenced just one step away from where we were, in Abbotsford, British Columbia. The finances were released and we stepped back onto the road.

First Fruits of a New Season

The first day in Abbotsford a few members of the team wandered across the concrete, graffiti-smothered slopes and embankments of the neighborhood skateboard park. They were headed out to walk and pray around the community before we started our evening programs. They prayed, "Lord we ask that you touch the hearts of the students who spend hours here on this site." Later in the day, a couple of those same team members wandered back to the park, which was now buzzing with the hum skateboard wheels and the crunch of slamming skateboard decks on obstinate pavement. Conversation was initiated with an easy, casual air, "We're part of the Bandwagon—that bunch of trucks over there," said the eager Upstreamers as they pointed in the direction of the unmistakable and outlandish addition to the students' familiar landscape.

Jeff, a stalky, athletic, high school graduate took an exceptional interest in the whole peculiar affair. He was powerfully drawn by the sincere love and attention that was coming from this unique crowd of God's ambassadors. Everyday after work, Jeff would hustle over to our Bandwagon and spend time building friendships, not hesitating to ask questions about the God we were introducing Him to. Within a week, Jeff had committed his life to Jesus and was prepared to offer himself to aid in our effort to get the message to more people across the nation.

The Abbotsford project was a difficult way to begin the new season. The churches there had been accustomed to working independently of one another and so our efforts in partnering with a unified church floundered. But Jeff seemed to be the evidence of God's first fruits—a small but valuable beginning to this new year of adventure with God.

Not by Sight

Now recall that I was pregnant and drawing closer and closer to the day of my delivery. How was it going to be on the road, uncertain of doctors, hospitals, delivery dates? Our next project was going to be 500 kilometers (approximately 310 miles) away in the city of Penticton. I kept consulting my home doctor, who was not far from Abbotsford—"Do I dare make the trip with just two weeks until my due date?" "You know," he cautioned, "It's possible that if you went into labor on the road, you might not make it to a hospital (it was two hours from one hospital to the next). You could be forced to deliver on a mountaintop and that's probably not a good thing considering your first delivery was a Caesarean." But the project was in full swing and Russ couldn't take the two-three weeks away from it to ensure safe delivery at home.

Every morning I was wide awake for no reason at 4 A.M.—I resigned myself to prayer. "God please provide the appropriate place for this baby to be born—help us to know what to do. Lord, give us the grace to live together with the new baby in this small space." God answered my prayers simply—I went into labor two weeks early, before the team left the Abbotsford area. There, in the same hospital where our other two daughters were born, with same doctor who delivered her sisters, Bethany came into the world. We even managed to have time to recuperate before we met the team in Penticton a week and a half later.

Lead On

If you've been keeping track, now we have three children. With my involvement in the music, leadership, and speaking, the two eldest, 8 and 5 years of age, were manageable—but a baby? There had been some help along the way but our prayers had been for the *right* person to aid us. I kept the feeling of panic pushed down and boldly exercised this new-found strategy of waiting.

Just a couple of weeks before the baby was due, God's gracious provision arrived in the form of a whole family—Marg, Jeff, Jason, and Kristina. They had become friends the previous winter—laughter and unceasing hospitality were served up whenever we were together, so we invited them to join us. They actually took us seriously, left the pastorate and arrived to join us in British Columbia—it was the answer to more than just our prayers. Jeff was keen to lend a hand to the overwhelming task of administrating our team that had swelled to 35. Jason, took on the responsibility of sound technician. Kristina had a natural affinity for our kids and jumped in to play with and care for the two eldest. And Marg lovingly offered to take baby Bethany under her wing for the evenings.

Bundled in the warmth of outerwear and blankets and strapped in the embrace of Marg's arms, Bethany experienced the first pre-winter chill of the evenings in the Bandwagon, peacefully contented and fiercely loved. She often fell asleep to the soothing sound of the Gospel in music and message and learned her early dance steps from the rhythm of Marg's constant swaying, even in the absence of music.

And so God went ahead, leading us across the nation, faithful in finance, faithful in project planning. One event would open doors to the next; divine appointments would secure unexpected opportunities; doors would close where the timing wasn't right. What we couldn't see—His strategy, His purposes—were the incessant reminder to lean into Him. Like children led through the darkness by a parent who knows the path well, His certainty became our confidence.

Chapter 6

Discovering the Power of the Name of Jesus

Canada, our "post-modern, post-Christian" nation has become chronically cynical about the Gospel. Like some verbal allergic response, our declaration of the name of Jesus has become the statement that we carefully dole out in tiny sampled tests to watch for reaction—but it is meant to be as essential as our life and breath.

This is the mind-set we struggled with when we stood in the venue of our very first Bandwagon mission. For three full evenings, we talked of reconciliation and the love of God and loving our neighbors, but were cautious of not saying the "J" word for fear of losing crowds (OK, so it was only 50 people, but it's all our egos had to bank on at the time). But then it happened…some bold, young soul said, "Jesus" from the stage and immediately, a disgruntled 40 percent of the crowd got up and left. Well there it was, rejection from our first assembly of Canadians—how could we go on?

By July of our second year, the Lord gave us a practical demonstration of the seriousness of what we were doing. It was the middle of the night in Penticton, British Columbia, and the team had just settled into their beds on a church basement floor. Justyn happened to be gazing out the window at the apartment building next door and in the haze of darkness witnessed the strange sight of two young men jumping off the second floor balcony of their apartment. He was quickly awakened to the reality that the building was on fire. Justyn immediately roused the team and ran with several others to the building to offer help.

Smoke and flames billowed into the night sky while numerous residents lay sleeping in their beds. Justyn, in his very proper British manner, knocked politely on the doors, calling gently to the inhabitants so as to not startle them unduly. He was shocked by the more intrusive measures the rest of the team was taking. "Fire!" "Fire!" shouted the Upstreamers as they ran down the hallways, banging on doors as they went, smoke choking every breath.

The heat and flames grew more intense and life threatening as Chris, Jay, and Derek reached the end of the final hallway—everyone had been warned and now the threesome needed to preserve their own lives. But pausing for a brief moment at the top of the stairs, they looked at one another, their minds echoing the same thought, "We can't leave without being absolutely certain that everyone is out." They turned on their heels and this time began to kick doors off their hinges in order to force their way into the suites.

Behind one door they discovered a woman sitting dazed and confused as her children ran circles around her, screaming in their attempts to search for the family pet, a bird. Jay frantically picked up one little girl and yelled for the others to follow him, which they did immediately. In another apartment, Chris and Derek found an elderly man, still in his underclothes disoriented by the chaos, and supported him out of the building to safety.

We were all sobered by this tangible example of our commission: the people behind the doors of our nation face real and imminent mortal jeopardy, and we, the Church, have the choice to knock politely or be willing to kick down the doors and say, "Follow me!" into the safety of Jesus' love and forgiveness. This, we are learning, is what we are created for—it is our act of worship to the God we love.

I'm Not Ashamed—No, No

But as extreme as this might sound, we have often sat poised to apologize for, more than we have been ready to defend, the hope that is within. Fear of man can be a more powerful motivator than our fear of God.

A local man looking in on the Bandwagon one day, had cornered Tamera partway through our presentation (he kept calling her "Camera" because she had said that her name rhymed with "camera" and he'd thought that was her name). "Um, Camera, why do you guys talk about all that Jesus and blood stuff? If you'd just keep all that stuff out, I think you'd find that people would be more willing to listen to your message."

Understandably true, though an impossible option—Jesus and His blood sacrifice are the very mystery of God's intervention to redeem humanity. Jesus himself faced the same response when His disciples declared, *"This is a hard teaching* [the body and the blood of Christ]. *Who can accept it?"* (John 6:60). And consequently, *"From this time many of His disciples turned back and no longer followed Him"* (John 6:66). Does Jesus need our help to improve His public relations? The Word speaks it plainly:

> *But these things are written that you may believe that Jesus is the Christ, the Son of God, and that by believing you may have life in His name* (John 20:31).

Salvation is found in no one else, for there is no other name under heaven given to men by which we must be saved (Acts 4:12).

It is the very name of Jesus that puts the power in our message. It is what sets our message apart from all the other motivational, self-help, and spiritualistic seminars that are competing for the allegiance of our fellow citizens. It is not a religion, or a philosophy, or a way of life, it is a person. A person, who unfortunately is as ridiculed in 20th century Canada and North America as He was in A.D. 30 when He was crucified. So why do we conclude that we, in proclaiming Him, will be any less unpopular?

In the Name of the King

The busy main drag of Penticton (July '96), with its passing crowds of vacationing students blaring their bass-booming tunes through wide-open car windows, is where the Bandwagon sat during the city's peak summer partying season. Our blatant declaration of Jesus may have seemed out of place to some, but we were a presence, reminding people of the Truth and prodding them in the direction of Jesus. Not many acknowledged Jesus' Lordship there, but I liken it to the work of the Royal Canadian Mounted Police early in our nation's history. In the name of the king, a lone Mountie traveled to remote places, among transient inhabitants, to maintain a presence of the king's rule.

Similarly, in the name of Jesus we proclaim His rule and sovereignty over the nation, regardless of the people's honor of Him (or lack thereof)—He is King of Kings and Lord of Lords; Jesus is Lord over Canada. Just as a lone Mountie has little personal authority, it is his representation of the crown that carries the authority. We are emissaries of the King, carrying His declarations, and He assures us with His promise, *"…So is my word that goes from my mouth: It will not return to me empty, but will achieve the purpose for which I sent it"* (Isa. 55:11).

He Who Rejects You, Rejects Me

Now, if you've not yet noticed, I have an odd inclination to live my life on the slippery slope of pessimism. Self-pity is the consequence of a God-test that I am choosing not to pass; it's a God-request, with an overdue answer that has slid into the swamp of unbelief. When a friend of mine used to pray for me, she would always get a picture of God putting His hand under my downcast chin, lifting it up. It's what He was doing with Upstream to encourage us to keep going.

After two anemic weeks of ministry in Vernon, British Columbia, (September '96), it was evident that the team was again discouraged. As we prayed for one Sunday night's program, Skye, a new team member, caught the dark tone in our voices and suddenly declared, "In Jesus name, I believe that many people are going to come out tonight to hear this message." We all looked at one another in silent apprehension, "But what if they don't come, then we'll feel really let down." But Skye was not to be put off. "We need to pray with expectancy! Let's pray for each of these seats—that the Lord would fill them!" We quietly complied, "Okay, if we have to…" (isn't it funny how self-pity always has that annoying whine to it). Laying our hands on the benches, we prayed that God would do what we were struggling to believe for. As day turned to evening and our program began, to our great surprise the Bandwagon was packed full. As a matter of fact, it was full from that day through to the end of the project a week later.

In general, the crowds in the Bandwagon were consistently inconsistent in size and response throughout our national trek. Spiritual dynamics and not popularity seemed to be the cause, as Jesus confirmed, *"He who listens to you listens to me; he who rejects you rejects me; but he who rejects me rejects Him who sent me"* (Luke 10:16).

His Name Changes History

The gorgeous mountainside town of Nelson, British Columbia, labeled by its native ancestors as "the Valley of Lost Souls" (where outcasts of the tribes were banished) was our next stop (October '96). The hundreds of street-dwelling youth (runaways from across Canada who called themselves the "Freaks" dressing and behaving as such) echoed the historic native label. In private and public places witchcraft was practiced; in farmers' markets cultic healing circles were common; in high places were altars to other gods; fortune tellers and all kinds of alternative lifestyles were the norm.

For centuries, this cycle of rebellion and rejection had gone on and discouraged local churches were struggling to overcome. Predictably, attendance in the Bandwagon was low, but as the early October snow began to fall and we took turns warming ourselves by a single fire in an oil barrel outside the tent, we had to believe that our declaration of Jesus was at least having an effect in the heavenlies. In song, through Scripture, and short plays, we boldly declared that the lost would be found by their Heavenly Father; we prayed it from the high places, on the streets, in public areas. We brought the love of Jesus to their doorsteps and asked if there was a need; we served free food in the Bandwagon as an act of compassion for the street-dwellers; we had numerous personal encounters on the streets.

On one, fogged-in day my daughter, Kezia, and I decided to wander the quaint streets of the town—she was unaware of the struggles we were having here, but a sudden declaration from this little ambassador made me think again. I had just purchased for her a unique little paper snake that was attached to a stick, its ceramic head-dangling out from a string connected to the top of the stick. As we walked, she swung the thing around making its accordioned body appear to writhe like a real snake and then abruptly remarked, "Hey this is just like Jesus."

Shocked and presuming that my 5 year old couldn't possibly have suggested the biblical connection of the two (like Moses holding up the snake in the wilderness; see John 3:14), I returned, "Now what do you mean by that, honey?" The confident preschooler responded, "Like the snake was held up on a stick, Jesus was held up so that people could be saved." Profound! And so with our prophetic symbol of Jesus in hand, we walked the pavement proclaiming that anyone who looked to Him (Jesus) would be saved from the sting of sin and death.

And what was the impact of all our activities? The town eventually saw several baptisms in the Bandwagon; but more significantly, shortly following our stay there: the "Freaks" began to disappear from the streets; there was less evidence of overt cultic and rebellious behavior; altars were knocked down; and many were coming to Jesus and returning to the churches. Today, the community needs another advance from the people of God to push back the darkness, but there is knowledge and a hope of what can be done in Jesus' name.

Lifting Jesus

Now, if our most powerful tool is the name of Jesus, is it not an exercise in futility that people get up and leave whenever we speak it? Here's what the Bible says:

> *Therefore God highly exalted Him to the highest place and gave Him the name that is above every name, that at the name of Jesus every knee should bow, in heaven and on earth, and every tongue confess that Jesus Christ is Lord, to the glory of God the Father* (Philippians 2:9-11).

My conclusion: if the name of Jesus causes every knee to bow and every tongue to confess His Lordship, then even the spiritual beings influencing a community will bow. Once the spirit realm is affected, the human realm with soon see a breakthrough. We may lose crowds temporarily if we declare "Jesus," but we will gain them back in the long term when spiritual chains are broken and people are freed to respond to His love.

We have even found that community parades and festivals can be places where we can carry out our declarations in public (and subversive) ways. At one secular business conference, our music team was hired to use our music to add landscape to the meetings. We sang about God's love and hope to the nation; we played "He is Exalted" and "Shine Jesus Shine" for their awards ceremony; we worshiped over them between their sessions. People so enjoyed it all; they even danced and sang along—"We are calling on you Lord…." One very anti-Christian man kept saying, "This is great—these guys do the kind of music that connects with the hearts of people." Another inquired, "What was that music you were doing during the awards? It really moved me!"

This is exactly what those outside the Church have been waiting for—it's the evidence that we truly believe in what we talk about. They want to know that Christianity is worth fighting for—that it is worth believing.

Interestingly, in communities where Jesus has been publicly worshiped through events, such as the March for Jesus, we have seen an immediate openness from unbelievers to Jesus and the Gospel. On the contrary, in communities where the Church sits silently behind their walls, the expression of Good News is like army boots trudging through thick mud—you get there, but not far and not fast.

So this has been our focus—we make sure that the name of Jesus is lifted up before the people as we worship because with so many other "gods" being worshiped in the nation, people need to know which one we're addressing. Further, it is an act that brings God's power and presence into our midst because, of course, we can't do any of this without Him.

CHAPTER 7

Bringing Healing into History

One of the more unexpected strategies that our team was quickly uncovering was the connection between the histories of communities and their present woes. Over the course of history, influences contrary to the God-ordained destiny of a place, obtain authority over the community and its inhabitants. It is Jesus' authority through His people that enables the breaking of ancient curses and, subsequently, the releasing of a community to return to Him.

The history of the sleepy British Columbian city of Greenwood is a fascinating collection of boons and mishaps. We took our time to research the place as we sauntered into its quiet midst in early 1997. Greenwood's initial implantation into the province was barely a thought as this town remained small and insignificant for many decades, but a sudden mining boom swelled its marginal population to a throng of 3,000 in a single year. The construction of hotels, an opera house, stores, and various other buildings instantly transformed the face of Greenwood's barren main street.

Yet as quickly as it flourished, the boom withered and within only a few years, the city went back to sleep. Decades later, during WWII, this diminutive metropolis lovingly embraced a new destiny as 1,200 interned Japanese, traumatically uprooted from their homes on the coast, were thrust upon the community. This new-found vitality kept the city prospering for decades, but again, as Greenwood's only industry, lumber, foundered and citizens sought work elsewhere, the wee beauty again fell asleep, this time unaroused by any new suitors. By the time Upstream arrived in the early spring of 1997 it was barely a village of 750—abandoned buildings and a struggling economy were the only remnants of its dormant history. But here God left a small miracle—a faithful pastor named Orville.

For 35 years Orville had committed to praying for God to awaken this place. He arranged for us to erect the Bandwagon in the vacant grassy field in the town's scant center, to bring life and hope to the town. Justyn declared to Greenwood: "Awake sleeping beauty from your slumber, your Prince has kissed you and has declared His love for you." Two men who had been asleep in alcohol abuse responded eagerly to the mysterious message—they were the first to receive the kiss of the Prince of Peace.

Traumatic events of the past and sinful behaviors are some of the ways a town can infect its history. Simply declaring God's divine purposes and His truths over a place can shatter historical curses, and residents who live those truths can rebuild new foundations.

Over the Mountains

The bleak, damp spring of 1997 found us in the small southern British Columbia towns of Grand Forks and Rock Creek, where we saw a flood of high school students accept the Lord and be baptized. As the spring thaw of our nation commenced, we hauled the Bandwagon trailers through the Rocky Mountain pass to our next frontier—the prairies. Good crowds and strong church unity made for a peaceful and prosperous project in Lloydminster, Alberta, and set a favorable course for this new season.

Just a few paces down the road is the historically charged city of North Battleford, Saskatchewan. On Canada Day (July 1, 1997) weekend, at a lakeside park overflowing with local residents, the Upstream team mounted the community stage as part of the roster of the day's performers. People were sipping beer, relaxing in the sun, only marginally acknowledging the entertainment. What were we to do? We weren't entertainers and this wasn't the Bandwagon. Did we need to mention Jesus?

Peace and boldness descended as we stepped to our microphones. We spoke of our mission across Canada, and the crowd applauded. Our clowns gave a hilarious demonstration of the gift of reconciliation and the people cheered. Then we declared, "It is by our response to be warriors for what is good and right that we can turn the tide of history and cause the broken places in the nation to be healed. And this, only by the power of Jesus Christ." Astoundingly, when our music team began to sing, faces in the audience lit up and many leapt to their feet to dance as though in agreement with our intentions for this town.

Uncovering the History

As part of home schooling our children we visited the museums and researched the historical annuls of each town. We discovered: how and when the town was established; significant historical events; tragedies; secret clubs; common ills and struggles; economic histories; current strengths; etc.—the lessons learned became the thrust of our prayers. In North Battleford, even my weekly haul of family laundry to the local laundromat allowed me to ingest the dynamics of the town. Interesting, on Wednesday afternoon, everyone who used the facility was of native descent (the racial make-up of city and surrounding area residents is comprised of 50 percent native-born Canadians and 50 percent Caucasian); but on Monday morning in the same laundromat, all of the customers were of white descent.

A brief look into North Battleford's history[1] educated us about the rift between native and whites. The area was originally established as a headquarters of the Northwest Mounted Police (NWMP) (later named the Royal Canadian Mounted Police) and was the sight of the infamous Northwest Rebellion in 1885. Louis Riel and the Métis of Saskatchewan were rising against the fledgling Canadian government and the native tribes had been prodded by the leader to join in the cause. Though the native leaders had firmly rejected the idea, seeking to honor their recent treaties, some of their young warriors, agitated by starvation and the negligence by the government, became embroiled in the battle. The non-native citizens of the town, terrified of the rumored native attack pressured the government to briskly deploy troops to aid in the conflict.

The Pain and the Proclamation

With rising fear and limitations of a small military force, the Prime Minister pressed the situation forcefully, publicly hanging nine men including Riel and several suspicious native offenders (the fairness of the trial was questionable), leaving the community reeling with shock. Prime Minister John A. MacDonald's declaration: "By this, the red man will know that the white man rules." Today, injustice and lingering pain have continued to cripple the community with mistrust and suspicion.

North Battleford was also the sight of the Latter Rain Revival in the late 1940s, from which church plants reaching as far as the nation of New Zealand have resulted. Regrettably, harsh disagreement among the revival leadership created two factions—eventually two denominations, and the whole thing came to a halt. After 50 years, the two churches were still at odds with one another.

With this history as a backdrop, we presented the message every evening in our Solomon's Colonnade to a small, transient, and unresponsive crowd. In an effort to at least affect the spiritual climate of the area, some of us set off to the native reserves to pray over the historical curses and pains there. We interceded for God's mercy where worship of other gods and other sins had taken place; we thanked the Lord for the many who had been living in righteousness; we went to where innocent blood had been shed and broke the curses; we prayed for freedom from oppression and anger. As God led, we prayed.

Through our research, we had discovered that there was a young chief called Poundmaker who had offered his life in order to stop the Riel battle. Poundmaker, innocent, had surrendered himself to the NWMP as a scapegoat on behalf of all the native people—he was victorious in his effort to halt the uprising, but not the hangings. Poundmaker's demonstration of Christ's sacrifice was a prophetic declaration speaking hope into history.

A Signpost

Shortly after our departure from North Battleford, God saw fit to encourage us. Harold, a team member, stood in an unusually long line for the toilet at the gas station nearest the Bandwagon, now parked in Swift Current, Saskatchewan. During casual conversation, he discovered that the group who had descended on the gas station were native youth from Arizona and had just been to North Battleford. They were an evangelistic troupe who used drama and testimony to talk to native young people about the transforming power of Jesus. When Harold told them that we had prayed specifically on the native reserves at North Battleford, they smiled. "We knew someone must've been there before us—it was so easy to preach the Gospel and there was a huge response from the youth."

Even more fruit—a year after our departure from North Battleford, we heard that one of the two churches that had split during the revival, approached the other and repented for their divisions. God brings healing into history.

Subversive to Submissive

The tainted history of Moose Jaw, Saskatchewan, the next stop on our journey, had a unique hold on this city. Calling itself the "Chicago of the North," Moose Jaw paid tribute to its exiled gangsters (Al Capone is said to be one of them), by offering tours in the tunnels under the city where they reportedly hid. Those historical pathways were affecting the city's current inhabitants.

Just before our arrival, we heard that 35 gang members had stormed into "Joe's Place," a youth drop-in center, and began to punch and kick Joe, the man who managed the center. He suffered a broken cheek bone, cracked skull, damaged spine, and a wounded heart. We had prayed immediately for God to intervene and turn the tragedy into opportunity.

He did. During the weeks of our programs, several of the students from the drop-in center, and even some of the gang members, wandered into the Bandwagon to hear the message of hope through Jesus—for many it clicked with the love that witnessed through Joe. Though there were no immediate responses from the gang members, several of their fellow students were publicly baptized and seeds have now been planted, historical pathways rerouted.

Similarly, Sheila, who had daily been visiting the casino beside the Bandwagon, was transformed. One night as I stood to make a final plea for people to stop playing games and turn their lives back to Jesus, Sheila walked by. She was on her way from the casino to the automatic bank machine to drain her account in a last ditch effort to get rich and cure her hopelessness. I saw her standing in the doorway, tears beginning to stream down her tired face. As much as she wanted to flee, she couldn't—instead, in an instant, she found herself in front of the stage, taking off her shoes to have Jesus wash her feet in the baptismal tank. "I want to give my life back to God," she wept. "I know that He is the only one who holds the solution to my life."

We observed it many times over: the miracle of God's presence with His people is the power that can break the curses of the past. His love, His healing, and the transforming power of His Spirit of Truth will change the very course of a community's history.

ENDNOTE

1. Arlean McPherson, *The Battlefords: A History*. (North Battleford: SK, Canada: Battleford and North Battleford, 1967).

Chapter 8

That They May Be One

At this point in the journey there was a rising of one conspicuously recurring theme: the unity of the Church. Simply put, we discovered that when the churches of a community love one another and are willing to work together for the sake of the Gospel, the message is believable. Jesus left us that message himself when He prayed:

> *My prayer is not for them alone, I pray also for those who will believe in me through their message, that all of them may be one, Father, just as you are in me and I am in you.... May they be brought to complete unity to let the world know that you sent me and have loved them even as you have loved me* (John 17:20-23).

As summer again turned to fall, we rambled north, to the petite rural town of Dauphin, Manitoba which sits at the foot of the unpretentious mountain slope of Riding Mountain, the subtle flavors of its Ukrainian heritage emanating from every morsel of this community's life. In this seemingly insignificant place God was doing a wonderful thing. Each week, there was a regular gathering of the clergy—they prayed together, they learned about each fellowship's beliefs and practices—and the impact that it was having in the town was remarkable.

Every year they publicly marched together under the one banner of Jesus and were, subsequently, fertilizing rich spiritual soil. When the Bandwagon rolled into town, we simply became part of what God was already doing in Dauphin. People in the crowded bleachers responded eagerly to every call we made—for repentance, for commitment and recommitment, for reconciliation, for baptism—person after person climbed in to be baptized, even until late on the final night.

Keeping Us Divided

It doesn't take a military strategist to figure out the best way to debilitate our skittish army of believers. Jesus knew that Divine power was bestowed through our unity—to render us powerless, all the enemy needs to do is keep us divided. Have we been blind to this obvious, very elementary battle tactic? How often have our fellow believers become the enemy? Is it possible for us to take a message of reconciliation to our nation if our greatest divisions lie within the church?

During our journey we witnessed too many church rifts to begin to recount, but one little church from another town serves as an excellent typical example. This vibrant community of believers had become our principal support as we arrived in their small town—they fed us, prayed for us, participated eagerly in the Bandwagon. But the project was painfully unyielding—people were elusive and reluctant to respond to our invitations; churches were disconnected from us; many seemed skeptical and aloof.

Then we discovered this one little church's connection to it all. It was not initially obvious since, as a church, they practiced the sign gifts (prophecy, tongues, healing, words of knowledge); they had powerful times of worship and sound teaching; they had deep fellowship with one another; and, lived simply so that their finances could be released for the work of God. But they had once been part of a larger fellowship—one that had been at the center of revival activity in the region. From the moment the smaller fellowship split off, the influential God-move fizzled out and the entire Church community was left shell-shocked.

Whether or not the unchurched of the community were aware of the division in the Church, it did seem to affect the receptivity of the unbelievers—few of them ever came and none responded to the Gospel. But that little fellowship began to understand—many of them came in public repentance for their divisions and have begun working toward reconciliation with their brothers and sisters from the larger church.

Forgiveness and Unforgiveness

Forgiveness: one of humanities greatest challenges. Histories of nations and wars boil down to this—and, surprise, the Church has not been inoculated against it. As a matter of fact, the people of God can manage to turn even a nasty root of unforgiveness into a righteous cause—rifts lingering for generations.

In the first year of our project, God made this point about forgiveness personal. We were sharing our plans to go across Canada at a local church and to my dread, at the back of the auditorium sat a man I had not spoken to for seven years. My heart leapt to my throat as a sweaty flood of fear, embarrassment, and insecurity swept through my trembling core. We had briefly worked together in a Christian ministry when harsh conflict arose between us. As a quick solution, the board had fired him and had peacefully left me secure in my position—an oppressive burden of anger and bitterness had lingered between us ever since.

And there I sat, as Justyn was calling the congregation to go to one another and reconcile. *"No one really has the guts to do this,"* I thought to myself as a wave of conviction struck my own heart. *"But I've got to go and lead worship... But Lord,* **he** *hurt* **me***...I didn't do anything...if* *there's something I did to him, tell me."* In an instant, a name came to my mind—a woman (a lawyer of all things) with whom I had shared my grievance those seven years ago, who had encouraged the board to fire him.

My knees shook as I walked to where he sat. From behind, I tapped him on the shoulder, mumbling, "I just wanted to say, 'Sorry.'" He wheeled around so quickly, I was certain I was about to get punched out, but he hit me with the opposite. His arms flung around me and his body was suddenly overcome by laboring sobs. Only his wife spoke, tears now streaming down her face as well, "You don't know what this means."

The effect of forgiveness is immediate, the act of it is simple, but it is regrettably underrated. We get convinced that it'll cost us too much, or that we deserve to be angry, or that *they* need to apologize first.

I have sat often with people who have shared with me the deep pain of abuse or of a spouse's infidelity or of relational damage. When the issue of forgiveness arises, hesitating, they say, "Yeah, I guess I need to do that," or "Lord, *help* me to forgive this person…." But I'll respond again, "He is already helping you, now *will you* forgive them?" There's usually a hopeful silence that I'll relent, but eventually with some effort and convincing liberty, comes the declaration, "Lord, I forgive them." That's it. The task is done. Freedom. Hooray!

The bad news is we've discovered that some of the most enormous pockets of unforgiveness reside in the Church. Why haven't we learned that,

> *…when you stand praying, if you hold anything against anyone, forgive him so that your Father in heaven may forgive you your sins* (Mark 11:25).

The Good News

Here's the good news. We've also observed that the shift in a community can be indisputably titanic when the church chooses to love one another—nothing can hold back the love of God through His people.

In the community of Powell River (September 1995) a young mother, a new Christian, approached the ministerial of the community to tell them that she had invited our team and the Bandwagon to come and naively asked, "Would you care to help out? They arrive in a week." Now in most places, her lack of planning ahead would be enough to provoke a series of "Don't-you-know-we've-had-our-church-calendars-planned-for-months?" guffaws. But here, where the pastors had been praying for a way to unitedly reach their community with the Gospel, the astonishing and unanimous response was, "This must be what we've been praying for—let's do it!"

The weeks that followed were the most exquisite dance of the Body of Christ—a building of one Kingdom only. Whether at the Bandwagon, in the local church, in the workplace, people were seeing the Gospel confirmed on every front and were dedicating their lives to Christ at all those places. One woman shuffled forward [in the Bandwagon], weeping, wanting to be baptized. When we called for people who were willing to support her in prayer, representatives from different churches lunged to the front—they had all been praying for her!

> *So neither he who plants nor he who waters is anything, but only God, who makes things grow. The man who plants and the man who waters have one purpose, and each will be rewarded according to his own labor* (1 Corinthians 3:7-8).

How Good and Pleasant

Unity comes from a focus on God's Kingdom—if we are focused on planting and reaping and harvesting to satisfy our own church growth tallies, we may discover the hearts of our churches and ministries to be competitive, jealous, and selfish. Our repentance of this behavior can immediately reverse those negative effects.

Such was the case in one of our west coast towns. Throughout this project there had been little response and interaction; few people in attendance; and, adding to the discouragement, the Bandwagon had been pummeled with vandalism, thefts, and verbal harassment. It has been said "the state of a community is a reflection of the state of the church of that community." Verifying this truth, we discovered that a silent war had been taking place among the churches—believers were moving from church to church so frequently that people were considering acquiring transit visas rather than bother with church membership. The baggage of animosity and unforgiveness was carried along with each petulant move and a trail of jealousy and suspicion was the only deposit.

In love, God led us in very direct ways to encourage these churches to confront their sin. They did. On a designated Sunday evening, in the town's theatre, the church members met for an impromptu joint service. A dozen pastors came forward and, with deep emotion, repented to one another for their divisions—the entire place was profoundly moved by this monumental event, many people weeping with their leaders, many hearts softened by the humble act.

The following two nights were evidence of the miracle in action—Bandwagon bleachers were filled to overflowing, the celebration exploded powerfully, and many people turned their lives over to the Lord. Further, those two nights just happened to fall in the eve of a potential national separation—the Québec referendum. The nation stayed together by a margin of only 51 percent to 49 percent. In other words, the church's choice for unity was perceptibly an act of intercession for the sake of the whole nation.

> *How good and pleasant it is when brothers live together in unity! It is like precious oil poured on the head, running down the beard, running down on Aaron's beard.... For there the Lord bestows his blessing, even life forevermore* (Psalm 133).

The Wheat and the Tares

Our historical study of another community unearthed the finding that whole areas of the city had been settled along denominational boundaries—the Catholics on the north side of the river; the Protestants on the south; the Mennonites in an area west; and the remaining marking out their territories accordingly. This innocent strategy was having disastrous effects on the potency of the church as a whole. As always, we asked the various churches to join together to proclaim the Gospel, but in their discomfort, attendance was irregular and people were standoffish.

At that time, our team was studying this passage from the parables of Jesus:

> *The kingdom of heaven is like a man who sowed good seed in his field. But while everyone was sleeping, his enemy came and sowed weeds among the wheat, and went away...Let both grow together* [said the master] *until the harvest. At that time I will tell the harvesters: first collect the weeds and tie them in bundles to be burned, then gather the wheat and bring it into my barn* (Matthew 13:24,30).

How often do churches refuse to work together based on "weeds"—differences in theology, in practice, in doctrine, in style? But weeds are rooted with good plants. When we leave it in the Lord's hands, then our responsibility is prayer: for more love; for greater understanding; for God's blessings on our fellow believers; that Truth will prevail.

As evidence to the fact, we heard that an evangelical church in the U.S. committed to praying relentlessly for their brothers and sisters in the World Wide Church of God, or Armstrongism. In just a brief period of time, the Armstrong group, once considered a cult, were touched by the Spirit of God, understood the errors in their beliefs and in one fell swoop, returned to the Truth of Scripture and to Jesus Himself.

For the community we were addressing, religious paradigms had paralyzed the flow of the Spirit of Truth and Love; prejudice had silently crept in through the back door and had barricaded the churches from one another. We prayed that God would bring to light these prejudices so the churches could lovingly be the Body of Christ to their community. Not much changed while we were in the community, but in the months that followed we received a letter from a woman that demonstrated more. She wrote that the churches were regularly crowding auditoriums for dynamic prayer and worship together, and God had revealed to them that the Upstream work had been a catalyst for the present victory.

Laughing Together

I have told you this so that my joy may be in you and that your joy may be complete. My command is this: Love each other as I have loved you (John 15:11-12).

With all the relational struggle I've attested to, it's hard to believe that our joy is somehow connected to this challenge of loving one another. When we come together in the power of the Spirit, He should fill us with joy to the point of hilarity, wouldn't you think? Perhaps it's what the gift of "Holy laughter" is all about—God releasing hilarious joy into His people.

One Wesleyan pastor "gets it." He announced to his congregation one Sunday that his love for Jesus was worth allowing himself a little humiliation to "leap like a calf out of his stall." In his fairly reserved church, it was a radical thing for him to suddenly get up and dance in the midst of worship—which he did. Then he carried it even further.

At the Bandwagon one evening, he challenged his fellow pastors, "You know, God has been doing an amazing thing in our community…I want the pastors to come to the stage with me and dance in thankfulness." Most of them kicked the dust in embarrassment, but a few jumped up and physically hauled the rest to the stage in a sudden burst of joy. Smiles and laughter urged them on as they threw themselves into the celebration, dancing crazy steps, swinging each other by the elbow—Anglican with Baptist, United with Wesleyan—undignified in front of their parishioners, egads!

Like David before the Ark of the Lord as it was being returned to Jerusalem, they worshiped with all of their might to the declaration:

> I will dance, I will sing, to be mad for my king.
> Nothing Lord is hindering this passion in my soul,
> And I'll become, even more undignified than this.

(From: "Undignified" by Matt Redman © 1995 Kingsway's Thankyou Music/MCPS)

Our "undignified" moments remind us of the feeble creatures we are when in the presence of the Almighty God. It is the common thread of our human weakness that pulls us together as we stand humbled before the Creator of the universe. We have misunderstood greatness and inaccurately presumed that by our beliefs, practices, and doctrines, we can somehow draw near to His greatness. No, on the contrary, it is in our humble state when He draws near to us, collects us together, our group, pathetic humanity, and lifts us up to bless and to be blessed.

CHAPTER 9

For Love of God and Neighbor

The Spirit of God is a persistent mother who longs for her children not to miss important life lessons. For us, this scripture was constantly prodding us—I believe it is at the foundation of our nation's struggle:

> *There is no faithfulness, no love, no acknowledgment of God in the land. There is only cursing, lying and murder, stealing and adultery; they break all bounds, and bloodshed follows bloodshed. Because of this, the land mourns, and all who live in it waste away...my people are destroyed from lack of knowledge* (Hosea 4:1b-3,6b).

Bringing the knowledge of God back into the land was the purpose behind the series of messages we developed based on the principles of the Ten Commandments—one per night. The skits, music, and spoken word all focused on the same theme—these became the essential handrails for a life of hope, freedom, and reconciliation—but they were not always the easiest messages to deliver.

Halfway through our project in Dauphin, Manitoba (August-September 1997), Justyn stood to present the evening's message: "Do Not Commit Adultery"—a challenging theme in a gender/generationally mixed audience. The team sat awkwardly staring at the ground accentuating the discomfort we all felt, as Justyn spoke, "Those of you who are involved sexually with someone before you are married are committing this same sin…pornography and other sexually perverse activities have broken your relationship with your Heavenly Father. I plead with you to turn from these activities and accept Jesus' gift of forgiveness."

Yikes! He just said it all! I imagined mothers grabbing their children by the hand and charging out of the Bandwagon, offended. But no one flinched; they all sat in silence, intent on Justyn's next words. "Why don't you come forward and we'll pray for victory in this area of your life." Uneasy, the music team stood to sing as people were given the opportunity to respond. Tension grew as no one budged. Then, as though a cord was pulling at hearts, one brave teenage guy came forward—an instant later, the front was crowded with people. Young teens stood confessing their involvement in pornography, lust, sexual activity—they all wanted to turn from these sinful choices. The young woman I prayed for sobbed as she admitted, "I've been dating a youth pastor and we've gotten involved sexually. I want God to forgive me for how I've wronged Him and I want to turn from this sinful behavior."

Make His Blessings Known

These messages were not consistently well-received—the "knowledge of God" is an education that places demands on its students. As proof, the reception our message was getting on the frost-bitten prairies that early October in 1997 was as bleak as the weather. We finished our Portage la Prairie, Manitoba, campaign and as soon as we could, packed up our rigs and headed home to British Columbia for a break, wondering: *"Do we carry on to the bitter end?"* With our motorhome roof leaking and incessant rain drenching us in our soggy trailer park locale, our aggravation was increasing. "Is this cost to our family paying off? Does the nation know God any better than when we first set out?" For our family, the answers were not coming.

Our return to Winnipeg, Manitoba in December set our commission rolling again. On the day we bumbled into a kids' drop-in center in the heart of the city, brisk air and snowflakes had just begun to fall, reminding us that it was nearly Christmas. The gathering of kids sat patiently, staring at us with dubious eyes as we scrambled to set up our instruments. Once accomplished, we clicked into gear with some familiar Christmas carols and a collection of other fun songs, and gradually, approving smiles appeared. My eyes scanned the room acknowledging each precious face—children from the poorest part of the city—as the words of the old Christmas carol we were singing unexpectedly gripped my spirit with an urgency of declaration:

> *No more* let sin and sorrows grow, nor thorns infest the ground
> He comes to make his blessings known
> Far as the curse is found…
>
> (From "Joy To the World" by Isaac Watts)

It was as though God was suddenly commanding us to stop the pain and devastation here and to faithfully proclaim that Jesus had come to break the power of the generational curses. *"Speak to these children. Let them know that they are loved. Let them know my ways. Bring Truth and Life."* In that short window of time, we did whatever we could for the sake of those children.

You Are Blessed if…

It is the Word of God that gets into our hearts and builds intimate relationship with the Creator of the Universe. Historically, it has been a strategy of the enemy to keep God's Word out of the hands of the common people. So it is the Word that we've needed to reinstate in hearts and minds so that, like the Psalmist, we can claim:

> *How can a young man keep his way pure? By living according to your word. I seek you with all my heart; do not let me stray from your commands. I have hidden your word in my heart that I might not sin against you* (Psalm 119:9-11).

The secret to presenting this "same old thing" to an inoculated "post-Christian" generation, is to turn it around. Not the "Thou shalt not(s)…" of the old covenant, but the "Blessed are those…" of the new covenant. "You are blessed if you live faithfully with one wife." "Joy will be yours if you honor your parents." "Abundant life awaits, if you choose generosity over greed." Included is the promise that God can heal and restore even when we've stepped off the path—perfect justice magnificently integrated by a bond of love with perfect mercy, that is our God. What better news could there be?

Our testimonies have often given tangible momentum to the message—who can ignore visible proof that living by the principles of God really works? In the audience one night was a man, Mark, who was being dramatically impacted by Upstream team member Tami's testimony, "My husband-to-be (also named Mark) and I are radically different, but God has been teaching us how to love each other with His unconditional love. It isn't always easy, but God continues to enable us." Mark from the audience shared, "My wife (coincidentally, her name is also Tammy), and I have been separated for some time, with little hope of change. I've been planning to leave the marriage entirely, but tonight I believe God can restore the love." After receiving prayer, he headed home to begin the work on his marriage.

Loving God and Neighbor

Jesus managed to sum up all of these principles in just two statements: *"Love the Lord your God with all your heart and with all your soul and with all your mind"* and, *"Love your neighbor as yourself"* (see

Matthew 22:37,39). Our team laid hold of these critical proclamations and took up our positions as ambassadors for reconciliation. As the apostle Paul expressed:

> *All this is from God, who reconciled us to himself through Christ and gave us the ministry of reconciliation: that God was reconciling the world to himself in Christ, not counting men's sins against them. And he has committed to us the message of reconciliation. We are therefore Christ's ambassadors, as though God were making his appeal through us. We implore you on Christ's behalf: Be reconciled to God* (2 Corinthians 5:18-20).

And our challenge is to steer clear of presenting the Gospel with any hint of condemnation—condemnation brings only the fruit of shame, striving, and hopelessness. The Spirit of God brings *conviction* so that people are compelled to respond to His love. Our commission is to love and serve.

This truth God dug into my heart on the day I sat with a woman who confessed, "I've been struggling again with the same sexual sin as before, but this time it's worse." In the criticalness of my heart, I cried out to God, "Why does she keep doing this? She's been through this before—she knows better!" I grumbled. "God I just want to give her a swift kick to get her back on track!"

An immediate voice of authority spoke into my mind, "You, Sandy, have been given a paved road to walk." My mind quickly scanned through my heritage of godly grandparents and parents who had shown me the path of righteous living early in my life. "She has been given a dusty road to walk" (she was the first in her family ever to embrace the Gospel), the voice continued, "How dare you condemn her for having dirty feet!" I began to weep as a wave of humility struck my soul. The commanding voice would not relent, "Get down and wash her feet!"

Sobbing, I turned to the woman and apologized for judgment that was silently going on in my heart. I took her hands in mine and began to honor her before God. "Please God, fill my friend with a deep understanding of your love. She has worked hard to try to do the right thing, but she's discouraged. I stand today Lord in the gap to believe that you can free her from this sin." We hugged and wept as God instantaneously restored hope.

This love from God, expressed through us, has the ability to provoke the kind of response a woman once expressed with a bottle of expensive perfume poured on the feet of Jesus:

> Precious Lord, here you are,
> Treading long rocky paths where my faith has been lost.
>
> Precious Lord, here you are,
> Covered over with the filth of my guilt and my shame.
> You've been walking my dusty roads.
> Released my pain and my past.
>
> Break this vessel and pour me out,
> Let my life leave the fragrance of love, your precious love.
>
> (From: "Precious Lord" by Sandy Rosen © 1995)

Chapter 10

Life in Community

Our vagabond life offered up another unexpected pressure—the taste of our fruit. The Fruit of the Spirit—those nine expressions of the character of Jesus in us: love, joy, goodness, gentleness, etc. can only truly be tested when the "bite" is on. Long hours, close quarters, limited time off, opposite personalities, an intense spiritual atmosphere—created a ripe atmosphere for relationally-evoked confrontations that exposed any and all bitter fruit. Hard to believe, but the tensions between us actually contributed to a process of pruning that enabled the growth of plentiful sweet fruit in our lives…if we managed to endure the process.

It was now two and a half years into the project and Myrtle, our motorhome that was initially a great joy to us, was beginning to exhibit serious road-inflicted deterioration and family growth limitations. Try as we may, a year and a half after baby Bethany arrived, we were struggling again to make life on the road manageable.

Our challenges were mounting. Maybe it was the fact that Bethany started to walk and was constantly dismantling her big sisters' belongings. Maybe it was the tedious battle to keep re-making our bedroom into dining room, office, homeschool room, living room, and back to bedroom again everyday. Maybe it was the fact that winter was approaching again and Myrtle wasn't capable of performing reliably in the cold. Maybe it was all the rainy days imprisoned in the motorhome while the roof leaked and we were exhausted, sick with the flu, and unable to escape the sound of each other's vomiting. Perhaps someone saw us starting to gnaw on one another.

Expanding the Home Front

For any one of those reasons, we began to cry out again for God to deliver us, struggling again to believe He would provide—we looked, asked, prayed, waited, and nothing. Our relationships were being stretched beyond belief and all sorts of ugly things were beginning to emerge from this oh-so-self-controlled woman. Impatience, anger…okay, rage—thoughts I never knew existed in my mind. God had definitely made a mistake. *"Why isn't he rescuing us?"*

He was. He was rescuing us from all those insufferable things that actually did exist in our hearts. In the easy seasons of life, I can mask the uglies, but they are still hiding under my skin. As long as life goes my way, I can keep them under cover; but presumably God allows the tough circumstances to linger long enough to let the bitter fruit come to the surface. Through tears and much repentance, I had to come again and again to my family, and to God, to apologize for my sinful responses. One of my biggest: unbelief. When things get tough, that's when I conclude that God isn't there—that He doesn't care about me. It's then when I begin to ponder on the great people of the Bible and wonder if they ever had my remarkable knack for doubt.

I look at Jehoshaphat's army (see 2 Chronicles 20)—God told them to send out the musicians as they faced a huge army. I can imagine being in the choir and looking for quick exits on the valley floor in case the singing didn't adequately soothe the enemy. And what about

Daniel? (see Daniel 6.) I wonder if maybe he started to sing, "The Lion Sleeps Tonight" using the power of suggestion as an alternative to the power of faith?

For me, I'm always looking for alternatives to trusting Him—I heard wrong; someone else did something wrong; God doesn't favor me; he's looking for me to "do" more. Lies all lies, distractions from the basic call to trust. For our family it was at our point of greatest desperation and greatest willingness to depend on Him, that God answered our prayers. His masterful miracle: just before reaching Winnipeg, Justyn and Joy sensed that God was prompting them to give us the new motorhome they had finally received. They would exchange ours for another, smaller one for them. Speechless and emotionally overwhelmed, we watched how God, with a single act, humbled us, birthed true thankfulness, and brought us into deeper relationship with one another, and with Him.

We Need Each Other

From my biology lessons, I know that one of the characteristics of living things is they respond to irritation. To live, we actually *need* irritation. So it wasn't surprising that more than a few times the exhausted, emotionally drained Upstream team sat grid-locked about some irresolvable issue. (Strange advantage of our vagabond life was we had nowhere to run from our conflict—we had to get through it!) Add to the mix, our diversity—the heritage of an Anglican, working with the dogma of a Baptist, thrust upon the ideals of a Charismatic, ruffling the stability of a Mennonite.

Forgive us dear host communities for our very unchristian-like behavior when we yelled at one another, stormed away in anger, argued for hours—all the while bringing a message of reconciliation! But let me push shame aside. By definition the dictionary says *reconciliation* is "a settlement or adjustment of disagreements, differences, etc."—there is no reconciliation unless we first have disagreement.

Learning Our Lessons

And there is no sin in allowing the disagreement to reside for a time as God does His work in each of our hearts. That terrible pain I feel until the situation is resolved is a stinging reminder to pray. By the time God has done the work in each individual, the problem may turn out to be something completely different from what we thought it to be, or often, the problem just disappeared.

One of our most impassioned discussions serves as a demonstration. Part of the team was longing for "more of the Spirit"—a common emphasis sparked by the Renewal Movement in the nation—and this longing arose at a team meeting. An immediate concern emerged from others on the team who feared that they would become obsessed with the experiential. As the discussion became more volatile, eyes rolled, anger erupted, and people stormed out—we'd obviously encroached on dangerous territory.

Should we have stayed away for the sake of *peacekeeping*? (I mean, we're supposed to be an example for the community, right?) No, I don't think so—we had stepped onto a battlefield where the Church has warred for centuries. As *peacemakers*, dealing with the issues now can settle the war for future generations. For eight solid, grueling hours we sat discussing, debating, arguing, listening, and praying—none of us allowed to skulk in selfishness or self pity. Gradually, as we began to hear and understand one another, we wept, we apologized, we comforted, we hugged—we reconciled.

Had anyone sat outside the door that day, they would've had serious concerns for our fitness to minister, but who said reconciliation is easy? It is in understanding the struggle for reconciliation and our inability to accomplish it on our own, that qualifies us to speak into the subject. If there were enough goodness in us to do the work of reconciliation, why would we need Jesus? It is the overwhelming nature of the process of reconciliation, that causes us to fall, humbled before our God, to call on his mercy and intervention.

It is apparent that since the inception of Church, we have been walking away from our struggles, leaving them unresolved and unchecked. I sat at a wedding recently, where mapped out seating arrangements were the bride's desperate efforts to keep the warring factions of her family separated. She knew that if they crossed one another's paths, there would be an uproar and someone would leave angry. So there she was, on the most glorious day of her life, tripping over boulders of historical grievances. May it not be the case for us when the Bridegroom comes to celebrate His wedding feast with us.

Love's Demands

How dangerous is honesty, how fragile is trust when relationships walk in fear. How firm a foundation is honesty, how strong a framework is trust when relationships walk in love. It was often that the undercurrent of our battles was fear—of one another, of the unknown, of the new, of intimacy, of being misunderstood. When we walk in fear, the pain that is actually bringing transformation can look like someone else's wrongdoing. Fear can produce seeds of mistrust, the weeds that choke the planting of good relationship. Derision and dissension become the pestilence of healthy community life.

But love makes one demand: that we live in intimacy and depth of relationship with one another, and be assured, sometimes it will be painful. But God allows the irritations of our life together to be the heat that separates the pure metal of Jesus shining in us, from the dross of our impure attitudes.

Getting Perspective

The barren snow-covered streets of downtown Winnipeg (now December 1997) were a good reminder that God had at least been merciful to us regarding weather. This hadn't been Winnipeg's usual flurry-and-ice-caked winter. But the weather was pretty much all we were willing to be thankful for at the time, in view of all the misfortune we had been plagued with since our arrival there.

Harold and Dave's vans were vandalized and everything of value—CD players, tool kits, bikes, etc.—was taken. Gus the bus wasn't working, so several times daily sound and musical equipment had to be loaded and unloaded into vans. Harold, our worship leader in lieu of Russ who hadn't arrived yet, was in bed, painfully ill with shingles. When Russ finally arrived, our new motorhome was vandalized and $4,000 worth of valuables was stolen—with no insurance coverage.

And then there was the flu epidemic that slammed half the team within just a few days (our whole family within seven hours)—fevers and vomiting running rampant. Things were not going well. Even our events were so poorly attended that we were convinced all of Winnipeg had been raptured. To make matters worse, we were in the midst of one of those very difficult relationship times with the team—it was the longest three weeks of our lives.

But in perspective, all of this was occurring in the context of the inner city, where losses are too numerous to count; where grief is so intense senses are numbed; where testimonies of shootings and deaths were shared with the nonchalance that I speak of a hangnail. For a time we let the interpersonal struggles get the best of us, allotting large portions of our day to work through team issues and struggling to get around to ministry. We were drowning in waves of grievances crashing on our heads and tumbling us in confusion, not letting go—of rights, of injuries, of justice.

And then Charles (not his real name), one of the few who come faithfully to our evening meetings, came shuffling forward to the microphone that last night. We had all noticed Charles silently sitting alone and disconnected in the expanse of the long wooden pew at the back. His subdued, stuttering voice was initially difficult to hear—our ears needed to be sensitized to this language of pain and deep grief. "When I was a teenager a gang attacked me and severely beat me. Just years later, I was raped by a man. My mother, my only family, died before I could talk to her about these things." His voiced trailed off as sobbing took over.

We all sat silenced. Our days of comparatively petty complaints—material losses, silly treading on other's toes, demands for "fair" treatment—was no pain in the light of real pain. The heat of the fire were experiencing was a weenie roast compared to this man's blazing furnace. We quickly let go of our grip on impure attitudes.

The Pain of Love

Strange that at the point when we conclude our relationships are awry, that someone is doing something wrong because there is so much pain, is the time when God is just about to give birth to something new. The moment that we say "I give up!" is when we can run, not away, but into the arms of His wisdom and understanding. God's plan is for us to live as brothers and sisters—friendship can be temporary, changing with emotions and life stages, but siblings are for life.

How much of the content of our disputes—some that can keep relationships paralyzed for years—are composed of the impurity of selffullness?

> *What causes fights and quarrels among you? Don't they come from your desires that battle within you? You want something but don't get it. You kill and covet, but you cannot have what you want. You quarrel and fight. You do not have because you do not ask God. When you ask, you do not receive, because you ask with wrong motives, that may spend what you get on your pleasures* (James 4:1-3).

The Lord knows we battle with our "self," our flesh. His solution:

Submit yourselves, then, to God. Resist the devil, and he will flee from you. Come near to God, and He will come near to you. Wash your hands, you sinners, and purify your hearts you double-minded. Grieve, mourn and wail. Change your laughter to mourning and your joy to gloom. Humble yourselves before the Lord, and He will lift you up (James 4:7-10).

Like Jesus, who laid down His rights we equally are being called to push through the pain of our relationships so His reconciliation, the true and peacemaking reconciliation, can be raised to life. It is the seed that falls to the ground and is buried that springs to become a fruit-producing plant.

We can comfort ourselves with this fact: it is the immature fruit that is so frequently bitter. To prevail through the drama of alternating seasons of isolating cold, persistent rains, and blistering heat, is to transform a chunk of tasteless flesh into flavorful, sweet fruit—fruit that will last and nourish.

Chapter 11

Overcoming and Battling

Nothing can adequately prepare you for the physical difficulties of traversing a nation. Loss, crisis, turmoil all seem to be connected to the challenge—for us it was connected to our vehicles. The temptation plaguing our human frailty is to give up in the battle, to lose faith in God's ability to guard and protect us, but He is constantly bringing us reassurance that He walks with us and that, in overcoming, we are being strengthened.

By January 1998 the team faced Ontario, Canada's largest province. The beauty of a Canadian winter is no better exhibited than in the spectacular scenery of Northern Ontario—myriads of snow-covered hills and evergreens dipping into the silent frozen lakes that separate snow lumps of islands by their pristine expanse of ice. The trans-Canada Highway remains hidden between towering snowbanks pushed up to the sides by snorting, salt-assaulting snowplows.

Winter is the giant in this land and our journey from Kenora to Thunder Bay will give you a taste of how ferocious the season can be, especially considering the entourage of decaying vehicles we had now accumulated. Here's the journal of an unusually difficult couple of days:

Monday

5 A.M.	Thermometer plunges to -30ºC (-22ºF), wind-chill makes it -40ºC (-40ºF).
5:30 A.M.	Russ leaves in courtesy van to pick up our motorhome which is being repaired in Winkler, near Winnipeg.
6:30 A.M.	Courtesy van breaks down leaving Russ stranded in the middle of nowhere—one hour away.
6:45 A.M.	It's *really* cold.
7 A.M.	Justyn locks himself out of his motorhome and waits for CAA (Canadian Auto Association).
7:30 A.M.	CAA arrives, unlocks the door and leaves.
7:35 A.M.	Justyn immediately locks himself out again.
7:40 A.M.	Our van won't start.
7:45 A.M.	Dave gets his van stuck in a snowbank.
7:50 A.M.	Our van finally gets jump started.
8 A.M.	Dave gets his van unstuck.
8 A.M.	Justyn leaves to run errands in Winnipeg in our van.
8:15 A.M.	CAA unlocks Justyn's door for Joy who has been left out in the cold.
10 A.M.	Russ is picked up by the repair company and continues on to Winkler.
10:15 A.M.	Heat not working in our van—it's still really cold!
11:30 A.M.	Justyn and Mark spin out into a snowy ravine and have to push the van back up the steep slope in the frigid cold.

Overcoming and Battling

4 P.M.	Mark and Justyn meet Russ at Winkler, in the unbearable cold, to unload equipment.
6:30 P.M.	Justyn and Mark finally return to Kenora.
8 P.M.	Russ returns to Kenora in the motorhome.

Tuesday

7:30 A.M.	Thermometer still at -30ºC (-22ºF) as team gets ready to leave.
8 A.M.	Preparing to leave, Justyn locks himself out of motorhome again!
8:30 A.M.	Harold's van and Kathleen's van won't start.
8:45 A.M.	Marg and Jeff's 5th wheel gets stuck on a hill.
9 A.M.	CAA arrives to unlock Justyn's *!-`*!….. door!
9:30 A.M.	Harold and Kathleen get van batteries jumped; Marg and Jeff get up the hill and all the vehicles finally get on the road.
11 A.M.	Heat no longer functioning in Rosen, Reuss, Popoff, Nisbet, Hartel vehicles and it's *ripping cold*!
11:30 A.M.	Pregnant Tamera switches to driving her own motorhome because the van she's been driving is too cold.
1:30 P.M.	Tamera switches to riding in Rees motorhome because her motorhome is *too cold*!
3 P.M.	Jamie and Julie's motorhome alternator dies and they are stranded in the cold halfway to Thunder Bay.
4 P.M.	Kathleen's van starts sputtering, but there's nowhere to stop, so her van sputters all the way to Thunder Bay.
6 P.M.	Most of the vehicles stagger in, but make it to Thunder Bay. Did I tell you how *cold* it is?

9 P.M.   Jamie and Julie finally arrive in Thunder Bay *chilled* to the bone.

Mechanical Casualties

Had our entire journey been reduced to survival? Our forefathers, thousands of them, in order to possess this land of promise, experienced the grace of God to endure their version of these similar difficulties. "Survival" is the word.

While driving the tiny main street of Portage la Prairie, Mark and Tamera suddenly noticed a lone trailer careening alongside their motorhome. "Hmmm, now that looks familiar." And then suddenly, "That's Georgia's trailer"! Which only moments before had been attached behind their motorhome. They pulled in front of it to stop its trajectory, thanking God that there hadn't been any major damage.

Twice Justyn and Joy were towing trailers that came unhitched in transit. Russ lost a trailer in the middle of rush hour on a busy city highway. I noticed the peculiar bobbing motion of his trailer as the tiny home on wheels careened across six lanes of approaching vehicles. I frantically prayed aloud, "Jesus! Help us, Jesus!" The stream of traffic stopped, and everyone watched helplessly as the trailer avoided several collisions before finally landing, undamaged, on the grassy shoulder.

Mark and Tamera's accelerator got stuck to the floor on the way into Grand Forks, British Columbia—they couldn't stop. It was the same day that a battery inexplicably boiled over in our van and the brakes gave out on Jay's van. Bob spun out on a rainy night with the highway tractor and Bruce and Donna lost the trailer brakes of their 5th wheel while heading down the steep incline of an enormous hill, but again, no damage. Dave's van slid out of control, spinning 'round and 'round on a snow-blown highway—his cargo of team members sat with the van's "look-at-that-it-ripped-right-out-of-the-floor" kitchen table firmly gripped in their white knuckles.

We've blown three transmissions, numerous alternators, and multitudes of other random parts, but God has been merciful to see us through and to keep us safe. Charitable mechanics and timely financial provision were our adventure's continuous miracles and God's affirmation that He was walking with us.

For the Sake of the Children

And how about our children in all of this? Should we stay clear of the battle for the sake protecting our families? I don't think so. A missionary friend of mine said it best when I questioned him about the safety of his children in the perils of South America, "There's no safer place for my children than in the center of God's will." Not only that, allowing our children to be exposed to the heat of the battle, we can train them up in their young years as warriors.

Our team is comprised of all the children of parents who've been battling in the nation for generations. Tony's parents have been pursuing French/English reconciliation. James' father did Jesus marches on the streets of England. Shiloh's parents have been involved in "on the street" outreaches with teams of children. Tamera's parents have evangelized among delinquent youth. Becky's dad is a renowned evangelist in Canada. Christie's mom has consistently interceded for the nation. Russ' dad promoted the cause of evangelistic summer camps. My mom and dad have involved themselves in evangelism and are currently ministering to the poor on the streets.

Most notable is Justyn's father who came from Britain and set off across Canada in the '60s, attempting to express the Gospel from east to west; but due to financial shortages and relational difficulties, he never finished the trek. Here was Justyn completing his father's battle more than 40 years later.

And God promises us this blessing:

> *Then our sons in their youth will be like well-nurtured plants, and our daughters will be like pillars carved to adorn a palace. Our barn will be filled with every kind of provision.... There will be no breaching of walls no going into captivity, no cry of distress in our streets. Blessed are the people of whom this is true; blessed are the people whose God is the Lord* (Psalm 144:12-14).

Training Our Hands for War

My children seemed to be getting it—it was even becoming part of their play. One day, I wandered into the forest at the historic sight of Stoney Creek, Ontario, certain my daughters had disappeared. From my vantage point on the crest of the hill, I could see, right there, a rustle of branches or, there, a flash of movement…for half an hour, like a sentinel at his post, I watched—I was hearing sounds but seeing no bodies and was preparing to set off to find them when all at once they appeared, breathless and smiling. They were, they informed me, pretending to be nurses scrambling to care for injured soldiers during their mock "War of 1812."

I was thankful that their history lesson for the day was taking root, but I was suddenly cognizant of how thrilling it was for them to be part of making their own history. On another day they were Acadians under siege and trapped inside Fort Louisbourg sending letters to France to plead for more guns. And again it struck me that what my children were treating as a game is actually part of their make up. They, like the rest of us, have been created with an innate sense of need to go to war for the things that we hold dear—our freedom, our future, our faith, righteousness. As David once wrote:

> *Praise be to the Lord, my Rock, who trains my hands for war, my fingers for battle. He is my loving God and my fortress, my stronghold and my deliverer, my shield, in whom I take refuge…*(Psalm 144:1-2a).

The Opposite Spirit

Since *"...our struggle is not against flesh and blood but against the rulers, against the authorities, against the powers of this dark world and against the spiritual forces of evil in the heavenly realms"* (Ephesians 6:12), then our weapon of war is to walk in the opposite spirit.

We arrived safely into Southern Ontario in the spring of '98. We set the Bandwagon in Waterloo, alongside the quaint St. Jacob's market on the outskirts of this busy and infinitely preoccupied University City. The stress and pressures of this thriving city are profoundly antithetical to the plodding and gentle Old Order Mennonite farmers who daily hauled their wares to market by slow-moving horse and buggy. It's there where we discovered the key to connecting with the harried people of Waterloo.

Our evening programs were well attended and enjoyed, but people were too fraught to take the time to really listen. Taking the cue from our black-clad neighbors, we took the focus off our busy program and set ourselves in the middle of the market—musicians busking and actors performing informal skits. The grassroots feel of this method seemed to jive well in this relaxed environment and people seemed more prepared to absorb it.

A young woman approached me after one evening program. "Hi, I saw you guys at the market today and I was really moved by what you were talking about. Could I ask you some questions?" For over an hour I answered her questions about life struggles and faith. Taking time from busy-ness had given opportunity for the Word of God to begin to take root.

This Means War

"Do not be overcome by evil, but overcome evil with good" (Romans 12:21). It is common these days for the church to talk about spiritual warfare, of tearing down spiritual strongholds. I've observed as people

have prayed them away, yelled them down, rebuked them, bound them; cast them out—all powerful and effective methods. But this charge, to walk in the opposite spirit, actually allows us to personally pull the plug on the power source of the enemy.

Our team understood this concept first hand. Repeatedly we would become affected by the spiritual dynamics of each community—if any of us had a weakness in the prevailing area of sin(s) of a community, it would begin to affect that team member. Our challenge: in order to bring the Gospel into that community, we had to first overcome that area of sin in our own lives.

My preparations to speak on marital faithfulness one night in a prairie town proved fruitless as Russ and I, unwittingly, locked into an angry scuffle. The intensity of it had us completely paralyzed as we limped into the evening program. No matter how hard we tried to hide it, the rift was evident. Determined to carry on with integrity, the two of us sneaked backstage while the program was still in motion and managed to apologize to each other.

We were at peace, but there was a strange, lingering resistance to the evening. We struggled to push the evening's message beyond the edge of the stage but our words virtually dropped to the ground as the crowd deflected our efforts to draw them in. Had our conflict ruined the whole evening? I don't believe so. More likely, as we found out later, the marital unfaithfulness rampant in that town, especially among church leaders, was irritating this area of weakness in our lives and it was the battle in the heavenlies that was bringing resistance to our message.

Using Spiritual Muscle

Please let me clarify this principle. Comedian Flip Wilson used to say, 'The devil made me do it"—this is not the idea here. Satan can't make us do anything. We struggle with the sin of our own lives—the spiritual strongholds of a community merely make that struggle more difficult. But overcoming it in ourselves actually wages war in the community.

I recall being on a short-term missions team where, as the team began to struggle with sin in similarly personal ways, the leadership would excuse it saying, "Oh, that's just because there's a spirit of _____ over this place." We dealt with nothing, and simply hoped we would survive the onslaught. But hadn't the Lord brought us together, as His warriors, to personally get a sense of the enemy, and to defeat him?

God is concerned with developing our spiritual muscle, through the overcoming of sin, so we can prepare ourselves to rule and reign with Him and join in overthrowing the enemy. Revelation affirms this: *"They overcame him by the blood of the Lamb and by the word of their testimony; they did not love their lives so much as to shrink from death"* (Rev. 12:11).

How To Not Shrink

An unusual common thread appeared in one quiet town where we were going door-to-door. People responded to us saying, "Oh is this a Christian thing? I'm not interested, I'm a witch," or "No thanks, I'm a pagan"—there was overt rebellion against God. Further, while wandering along a railway track, the team found altars for the worship of all sorts of spirits contrary to the Spirit of God. Though the churches of the town were aware of the presence and meaning of the altars, they took no action for fear of consequential curses. They didn't understand that we possess the authority of Jesus Christ with which the power of every curse is broken.

With this knowledge, our railway-track-wandering team began to kick down and demolish those altars proclaiming, "Jesus Christ is Lord" from that high place. Other members of the team, equally stirred by unusual boldness, stood on the street corners of that town, worshiping Jesus and speaking aloud the Scriptures. As bold as some locals were being in their defiance, the Upstreamers were being fearless in their obedience.

Fear is how the enemy manages to paralyze us—he thrives when we don't reclaim places where he has been given control. This is why there is such great power in *not love(ing) our lives so much as to shrink from death*—dying to what is important to us so that we will not be tempted by the fear of losing them, be it friendships, reputation, career, future, finances, anything. Like Abraham laying his future, Isaac, on the altar (see Genesis 22), laying down our rights to things of importance, facilitates obedience and prohibits the snare of our enemy.

Stepping Out

All of this power is not just for "those who have a special gift to do those kinds of things." We Upstreamers are nothing but very usual people with very usual temperaments and abilities. Georgia, who stood speaking out Scripture on the street that day, resisted her normally gentle, inoffensive manner and began to read aloud. First, in a barely audible voice, but then something welled up in her and she began to speak loudly, even shouting out the Word of God. Oblivious to the stares of passers-by, her apprehension had been eclipsed by a more powerful fear of God and the motivation of the Holy Spirit.

When the character and reputation of the one true God are being trod underfoot in our land, how can we sit idly by and permit the enemy to advance? Never in the history of the nation has there been such intolerance for truth about God; never has there been such a disdain for righteousness. I heard a well-known TV journalist say, "The first casualty in the war for political correctness is truth." The dance of us keepers of the peace is nothing more than a tango with pride and fear of man—we may risk stepping on toes, but our Truth-starved world needs to hear Truth. Samuel warned the people, *"Be sure to fear the Lord and serve him faithfully with all your heart..."* (1 Samuel 12:24).

Disarming Distraction

Now, getting back to Waterloo, from there we shifted just a short distance to the small town of Hanover (May 1998), finishing a thriving project here (see Chapter 17). By the end of June we arrived north of Toronto in the city of Orangeville. Distraction and apathy are what seemed to keep this community of commuters spiritually numb. Our program was climaxing one Saturday evening and the crowded Bandwagon seemed oddly electric with anticipation—a steady stream of wandering townspeople were peeking in and people sat perched on the edge of their Bandwagon seats as Justyn began to share a powerful message of hope and peace.

Without warning, his voice was instantly obliterated by the shrill scream of an ambulance siren. He grinned as he paused, and then carried on once the sound had dissipated, but was interrupted by the noisy entrance of a drunken man. Children were suddenly galumphing their way up and down the theatre stairs; in the doorway, two bear-like dogs leashed to a woman began to yelp; and, heightening the cacophony, a parrot on a man's shoulder began heckling our already fraught evangelist.

Now one solution to this encounter with chaos would have been to vent all the frustration boiling in Justyn, with a blast of, 'Would everyone please be quiet, I'm trying to share something very important!" Instead Justyn remained in a state of peace and patience, responding with humor to the heckling parrot, and carrying on with Jesus' message of hope that carried its own ability to compel its listeners. His response in the opposite spirit seemed to defuse the power of the distraction and apathy, and that night many were inspired to commit their lives to the Prince of Peace.

Responding in Faith

But our enemy has his plans to even knock this strategy off the rails. From Orangeville, we moved to the small town of Lindsay, Ontario (see

Chapter 17) and by August we arrived in the city of Peterborough. A difficult project here had finally culminated on the last evening with powerful worship and a collection of meaningful baptisms. There, reclining in the doorway of our Solomon's Colonnade, was Mike, a husky 30-something man in a wheelchair, grinning as he savored the unique sampling of joyful energies. One of the team understood from his hand gestures that he was deaf and couldn't understand what was going on, so the Upstreamer grabbed, Julie, a team member trained in sign language, who began by written note and hand signs to boldly communicate the message of salvation to Mike.

Mike smiled big as he wrote, "My sister from Thunder Bay worked with you guys and she told me about your project. Her name is Meredith." Immediately recognizing the name, Julie gushed, "God must have orchestrated this." Mike wrote that he wanted to accept Jesus—Justyn led him in a prayer for salvation and planned to have him return later because he also wanted to be baptized.

The team had just been studying about the miracles of Jesus and were challenging one another to believe for miraculous physical healing—Mike was a sign! God wanted us to walk in the spirit opposite to our own unbelief and have faith for Mike's healing. He agreed to let us pray for that and returned after the crowds had dispersed.

Apprehensive but determined to be obedient; the team began to pray for Mike's hearing. Fingers were placed in his ears and words of declared healing were breathed into their deafness. In just a few minutes he heard Russ' guitar—everyone rejoiced. Without hesitation, a hand was placed on his mouth and a command for speech was uttered. Mike instantly strained with deliberating tongue to speak, "Je-sus," and the team was giddy with amazement as they applauded God's miracles.

Bowled over with joy, we kept on and prayed for his limp, lifeless legs—the limbs began to quiver and shake as prayers exploded in confidence. Tears and shouts of glee erupted when his wobbly legs pushed

Mike up, teetered to standing as he took his first steps. Everyone cheered as he walked, then jumped unaided across the dusty floor of the Bandwagon, eventually carrying his wheelchair over his head. Our excited team continued celebrating until well into the night and our joy lingered through the next days.

The warmth of euphoria remained until two days later when Julie and her husband, Jamie, called from Thunder Bay on their way back to Alberta. "Healed" Mike had given them his sister Meredith's phone number and they called her. Meredith's innocent words were an iron ball against hearts of glass, "I don't have a brother...." Jamie and Julie were frantic for us to try to connect again with Mike. All of our efforts were fruitless—he wasn't where he said he was living; the wheelchair was a loaner from the local drugstore; no one in town seemed to know him at all; even his "sister" could only conclude that he may he been a foster child in her home, but his name wouldn't be Mike, and his handicaps wouldn't have been real. Our conclusion: we'd been duped.

Believing for Provision

We arrived in the next town, Hamilton, shell-shocked and barely able to continue. It was September of year four and we had just experienced our first serious mortal wound from the battle—the whole of the Upstream team languished between faith and unbelief, losing purpose and direction—all of our reference points had been turned upside down.

Doubt is connected to a fear of failure, but its opposite, faith, is connected to a faithful God who has already won the victory. He can be trusted; He will never fail us. So it was in the thick of our despair that Dave stood at a team meeting to encourage us with the song "My Deliverer is coming, my Deliverer is standing by..." It was God's promise that He would continue to be with us and rescue us from the plight, the fear that our vagabond life was bestowing on us.

For Mark and Tamera, they had no choice but to step out and face their next frontier of challenge—the spirit of fear of provision. They were about to have a baby thousands of miles from home. Tamera remained peaceful and believed for God's provision for the birth of the baby at just the right time and in just the right place. God's promise to go ahead of them was demonstrated not only in the provision of a motorhome and a doctor in every town where we resided that summer, but also in the remarkable delivery of the second little on-the-road baby, Abigail, in the hospital-rich city of Hamilton. God had even made provision for grandparents to be there, cheering from the sidelines.

It is clear that this fundamental strategy of battle, opposite spirits, has profound effects. If fear is present, express the love of God; if there is greed and selfishness, live out generosity and selflessness; if there is lust or infidelity, exhibit unconditional love and faithfulness; if anger and rebellion reside, seek to walk in peace and honor for authority. In this way, the power of the kingdom of darkness is attacked and debilitated, and the Kingdom of light advances.

Chapter 12

"Everywhere We Set Our Foot"—Claiming the Land

Oh, the lessons we have learned. Let me pause for a moment to give you Upstream's top eight things to beware of while traveling in the nation of Canada:

#8 Never eat Chinese food at a truck stop in a rural prairie town.

#7 "Butte" is a woman's last name and is not to be used to address the woman.

#6 Tupperware is useful for everything, even dumping motorhome sewage.

#5 Never sing, "This land is your land, this land is my land" on a native reserve.

#4 "La toilet de ma grande voiture est trés fatigue" ("The toilet of my big car is very tired") doesn't mean, "Where is your sewage dump station?"

#3 You may not be able to take prayer seriously again if someone gives you a bright blue nylon hat with "Prayer Warr**oir**" printed on it.

#2 All potato salad is edible, even if it's purple.

#1 When staying in a rustic cabin, make sure the snowbank you relieve yourself on is not used for drinking water.

Every Place You Set Your Foot

It is an imposing journey to travel the huge expanse of Canada—the second largest nation in the world. So why the odd compulsion of the Upstream team to be doing this project by land? *"I will give you every place where you set your foot..."* (Joshua 1:3) was God's promise to Joshua and we sensed the same was true for us. Our forefathers had dubbed us as the *"Dominion of Canada,"* as a declaration that, *"He shall have dominion from sea to sea; from the river to the ends of the earth"* (Psalm 72:8). But many other spiritual authorities, like squatters on abandoned properties, have, through the decades, claimed dominion over the land—we needed to claim it back.

Now how does "claiming the land" really happen? As the Royal Bank commercial says, "One Canadian at a time." Jesus lays out clearly that we must make disciples—but how do we find them? Jesus acquired them in the marketplace, by the sea, on the streets, in the synagogues. But how do we translate that into the insular, private lifestyles of North Americans? In a culture where we can now shop at home, work at home, get exercise in the home, even have church at home, how do we overcome the dilemma of making personal connections with would-be disciples?

It was Justyn who knew and dragged us (Upstreamers and locals) to the doors of our neighbors' homes in every community to discover the answer. This intimidating exercise was a fearful/wonderful leap out of our comfort zones and a strategic tactic, bearing some of the most dynamic examples of a compassionate God carrying out His practical work. This is the interactive part of walking the land—to go behind the barricade of the front door and into the fortress of the home. And what have we discovered? Loneliness, hunger, pain and anger, hopelessness, indifference and unanticipated openness.

What Do You Want God To Do for You?

Before we began each of our formal programs, we spent two or three preceding days knocking on as many doors in the community as possible. This gave us the chance to invite and pray with our new neighbors; it also gave us a sense of the spirit of each community.

Kathleen and I began our door-knocking in one of the city's middle-class, suburban neighborhoods. While going from door to door, we noticed a middle-aged man across the street who was working in his yard while glancing uneasily in our direction. We finally arrived in front of his home where he boldly confronted us, "I've been watching you. What kind of church are you from?" We gave a brief, nervous explanation of our mission to the nation and of our involvement with local churches and paused, awaiting rebuke. But the look on his face was an unexpected overwhelming grin. "All the other cult-type groups have been out here, it's about time the Church got out to the streets," he said as he shook our hands. "I applaud what you are doing!"

It's true. The hunger, sadness, and pain behind the doors has for far too many decades been fed by one sort of deceptively appealing cult group after another. We know the Bread of Life, it's time we shared it.

> Arise people of the Lord feed the hunger of the nation.
> Arise let the love of God restore ignite a flame of revelation.
> May your Spirit be released and the pow'rs of evil breached.
> Revive the hope in the hearts of the people.
>
> Traveling through the Rocky Mountains,
> Journeying over prairie plains,
> Knocking on doors and finding only famine.
> Hungry for the Bread of Life,

Thirsty for the Living Water,
Asking for more than empty religion.

(From: "Arise" by Mike Priebe & Russ Rosen © 1995)

The point of door-to-door is not conversion; it is to begin a simple introduction to God. Our main question, "What do you want God to do for you?" is the same question that Jesus asked the two blind men (see Matt. 9:27), the invalid at Bethesda (see John 5:2), and Bartimeus (see Mark 10:46). The idea is to get people talking to the One with whom the relationship really begins—a God who already knows them by name. He does the rest.

Doug met us at his door—his straggly hair, rumpled muscle shirt, and tattoos made for an intimidating first impression. I noticed the large tattoo on his upper arm had a face, the name "Sandy" and a date. "What's that?" I inquired, daring to point at the curious tattoo. "That's my brother, he was only 15 when he died—his death was all my fault." Doug's eyes brimmed with tears as his two young children suddenly appeared as if in rescue. "What would you like God to do for you?" we continued. "Oh just to keep our kids safe…" he cautiously offered. They're on his doorstep, as we prayed for his children, we also slipped in a prayer that God would meet him in his grief and bring healing.

Knock Knock

Sometimes the needs of a whole town can come spilling out the doors. One town gave us an exceptional and immediate sampling of its ailing heart. Upstreamer team member Dave and a member of one of the local churches walked along the aging streets to knock on the doors of nondescript homes. One woman agonized, "My boyfriend recently committed suicide and my house just been burglarized." They paused only briefly before boldly offering, "Only Jesus can help you!" "Yes, you're right," she resigned, allowing their prayers and their introduction to God.

At the next door, the same pair encountered a middle-aged man who, in an instant, disclosed that his wife had just left him and that he was frantic with despair, entirely unable to discern what to do next. Dave and his partner began to pray for the desperate man. Overcome with unfettered emotion, the man began to weep, hugging them and thanking them profusely for their prayers.

Georgia and Louis found none of the doors open in their assigned area, so they conceded to stroll the streets. "What do you want God to do for you?" they inquired of a young woman who was in tears. "My husband just left me this morning for one of our neighbors." (Apparently a common theme here.) The team members joined with the woman in taking her sorrow to her Heavenly Father.

Moments later, a biker gang parked themselves opposite gentle Georgia and shy Louis. In a burst of boldness, the two approached the gang and questioned, "We are concerned for this community and we were wondering what you would want God to do for you?" Instead of the anticipated laughter and ridicule, one burly man held up a tattooed arm that was obviously injured. Without fear, and encircled by the tall husky bikers, Georgia and Louis inaugurated an impromptu prayer meeting for the man's healing—who would've thought.

Wendy prayed for a man whose brother was in a coma. Justyn prayed for a woman's concern about the theft and violence among the teens. Maurice prayed for a woman's ill daughter...the testimonies went on and on that day. It was an astounding illustration of how crisis can bring people to the foot of the Cross and how our personal involvement intersects as a road sign pointing in the direction of real hope.

Divine Appointments

Why God has chosen to allow us to be part of His relational equation is a mystery, but there is no doubt that we are sometimes the knuckles with which God raps on a door. Like Philip to the Ethiopian (see Acts 8:26), or Peter to Cornelius (see Acts 10), our obedience to go to a door, may actually be part of God's miraculous provision.

In February of 1996, we heard there was a tragic murder in Campbell River, a town that we had just ministered in. A young mother had been brutally slain by her live-in boyfriend and her three grieving teenagers had been left the mire of the horror. We prayed immediately for her despairing children and for their painful, fractured lives.

It was several months later (July '96), and hundreds of miles away in the city of Penticton, when two of our team members knocked on the door of the home where a lanky teenager, Matt, was staying. "Hi. We're visiting your town—could we ask you some questions?" "Oh, I'm not from here," Matt said, avoiding eye contact. "So where are you from?" "Oh, I'm from Campbell River. I've come to live with my grandmother and my father." "So why did you come to Penticton?" the two prodded. "Because my mom was murdered last winter in Campbell River." This was one of the teens we had been praying for!

Recognizing God's divine appointment, we took Matt under the team's wing—serving him meals, spending time with him. And on the day we prayed for him, the well of unwept tears finally burst down his grief-etched face as we pleaded for his Heavenly Father to bring comfort and healing.

We soon discovered that our connection to Matt went even further. He arrived early on the day that we were setting up the Bandwagon and as he approached the trailers, distinctive in their color and design, his eyes lit with immediate recognition. "Hey, I know you guys! I was there on Halloween night in Campbell River! Me and my friends were dressed up and…" He paused, realizing the embarrassing fact—he had been part of the ghoulish crowd that had pelted our theatre with eggs that night. Redemption…God healing the past.

Can a mother forget the baby at her breast and have no compassion on the child she has borne? Though she may forget, I will not forget you! (Isaiah 49:15).

God Is Here

To walk the land with personal contact dispels the myth that, "God is watching us from a distance." On the contrary, He is very close, wanting to touch us individually, personally, and intimately. Getting people connected to this kind of loving God is revolutionary and transforming.

"We don't have to do that part, we should just carry on up the street," I weakly proposed, as Kathleen and I considered the cul-de-sac ahead in a dry Cambridge, Ontario neighborhood. "Aw, let's just do it anyhow, we've got time," Kathleen retorted. And so we knocked on the doors around the circle, only to be met by curt, uninterested youth. "We shouldn't have bothered," grumbled my thoughts, "Why do we do this anyhow? Thank goodness, only two more to go." But this encounter would make a difference.

Lisa, an attractive young mom in her 30s, opened her door. We quickly rattled off our too-familiar discourse about the Bandwagon and praying across Canada and "What do you want God to do for you?" inwardly preparing ourselves to move on to the final door. But the woman burst into tears. We stood in bewilderment as she fretfully squatted at her daughter's feet to put shoes on the 3 year old. Struggling to get the tears under control, she followed the tot out the door and we mutely paraded along behind, unprepared to let this opportunity pass us by.

The three of us stood hushed on the clean black asphalt of her new driveway. I waited only a moment before I again dared to forward the question, "What do you want God to do for you?" Lisa cautiously began to pour out her heart, tears flooding from her eyes afresh. "It's been a really rough year in a new neighborhood, a difficult marriage, and incessant business demands. I've felt so hopeless. Do you know that at exactly one o'clock today I prayed, 'God if you're there and still care about me, will you please show me?'" She erupted into sobs as we all internally concluded the obvious—it was now four o'clock and we stood before her asking, "What do you want God to do for you?"

Intercession for the Community

It would be great to say that every connection had a similarly significant response—that every conversation provoked tears—but it wouldn't be true. The Church still has work to do. James and Georgia were greeted by a half-clothed man, still foam-bearded for his morning shave. Hospitality took sudden priority and the man immediately invited them in, oblivious to the inconvenience of the moment. "So what do you want God to do for you?" came the question. "Well, a cure for AIDs would be nice," the man said bluntly. "I'm HIV positive."

He continued, "I used to go to church, but when I was honest about my homosexual lifestyle, I was ostracized. The people in the church used to pray for my healing from it, but I never was. Now I choose to believe that God loves me for who I am. If I couldn't believe that, I'd be completely hopeless." A tone of bitterness filled his voice as then he said, "No, don't bother praying for me. If God wanted to heal me, He would've done it already." Compassion and grief filled James and Georgia as they silently returned to the door—what could they say? Outside, walking the path from the man's house, they simply lifted him in prayer.

In another town, our conversations with the street-wandering students exposed the heavy cloud of pain over them. The recent suicide of one of their beloved buddies had left a muddy residue of grief and disillusionment. Regrettably, their greater anguish had come from the young man's funeral proceedings. During the memorial service a local pastor had innocently mentioned, "It is a sad choice that Nathaniel made, but God didn't intend for him to die this way." Their conclusion: the pastor was blaming their deceased friend and so they turned their bitterness toward every church in the city. We could only pray—for hope and healing; for forgiveness and reconciliation.

Land Claimed

> In this dominion from sea to sea,
> We pray for mercy Lord, for the true north strong and free.
> Release your spirit of love and hope,
> Revive our vision 'cause we're calling on you Lord.
> We're calling on you Lord.
> This is my country, this is my home.
> I love my country from east to western shore.
> I'll not be shaken, I will stand sure.
> I'll walk the land and hold your hand until there's
> unity once more.
> This is my Canada, my great big Canada, beloved Canada,
> This is my home.

(From: "This is My Country" by Russ Rosen © 1995)

There are hundreds more stories to be told and the common theme in the prayers, the declarations, the worship in His name, the love expressed, the lives reclaimed, is that God is releasing this nation into His loving grip. As one woman very profoundly declared to us one evening after we had sung this song, "God claims: 'This is my Canada, my great big Canada, this is my home!'".

CHAPTER 13

Seeing in the Unseen

Undoubtedly, one of the most confounding constants everywhere we went was the evidence of spiritual realm touching down in the natural—events that were well beyond our human comprehension; circumstances that, like Jesus' mother, we were left "pondering." For me, the whole sphere of the supernatural and of dreams and visions is completely unfamiliar territory.

But since God is Spirit and He speaks to our spirits in ways that are spirit-sensitive, the weird and the wonderful realm of the unseen sooner than later exposes itself. God sets up street signs along the road of faith—assuring us of our direction, or confirming something that He has already spoken to our spirits.

We experienced some dynamic examples of these street signs early in our journey. The Indian summer sunsets of Powell River in the fall of '95 gave way to a deluge of torrential rains. With no roof and no refuge from the depressing dampness, the team sat huddled cross-legged on the floor of the stage trailer in strategic groupings to avoid the drips that blew in from the front ledge of the trailer and the others that dive-bombed from the holes in the ceiling inside. Our daily Bible study had just begun when Christie suddenly looked up...and around... "Does anyone hear that?" We all shrugged. "Can't you hear it?...I hear angels singing!"

As a team, we were all still getting to know one another—Christie didn't seem delusional, but as hard as we listened, we couldn't hear what she was hearing. What could be the meaning? Though we are uncertain, we know that that mission in Powell River produced enormous fruit—many, many people responded to the Gospel—perhaps the singing was in celebration.

The Heavens are Speaking

Sometimes God spoke to us through multiple avenues to get our attention on a single message. During yet another stormy fall project, the wind daily howled through the Bandwagon, sheets of incessant rain sliced the air and a demoralizing squall raged. Not a day went by that the gloomy wet breath of the elements didn't torment us in this seaside town. The physical and the spiritual both seemed to be exhibiting signs of unrest and turmoil.

Here, people had made offerings to other gods—idols and symbols of their worship were set up in public places. Here, the churches were struggling and the Bandwagon project was symptomatically a difficult one—but our team was at a loss for guidance. Many of the team awoke nightly, mostly to pray, but some were having vivid and meaningful dreams and visions.

I had begun to experience a strange phenomenon in the night—I would be awakened from my sleep but as my conscious mind was still coming to, my subconscious, my spirit, was already praying. My spirit was in battle, praying for protection, taking authority in the name of Jesus—all before my body and mind were physically awake. How and why was this happening?

Kathleen dreamed of a swimming pool that, oddly, had water only in the top half. A piece of raw meat lay in the bottom half of the pool and she heard someone say, "The meat is the flesh and the water is the Spirit. See, they don't touch, they don't touch at all." Was this a reminder to stay better connected with the Spirit of God and not attempt to accomplish things in our human effort?

Kezia, our middle 4-year-old daughter, also had a dream at this time. "We were all climbing up to the top of a statue of Jesus, but when we got there—turkeys! There were turkeys everywhere! The turkeys just kept bugging us." The strange little dream was disturbingly profound. At every turn on this project, there had been bothersome incidents—illness, relational struggles, weather, crowds (the lack thereof), and vandalism. Her dream confirmed that these things were distractions, just turkeys bugging us, things to discourage and take the focus off Jesus.

Yet another team member had a vision that her arms and legs were heavy planks of wood with "Jesus Christ is Lord" written on each. They were being raised up as a building, but they didn't have "dovetail joints," so they would come crashing back down. The team member couldn't move her physical body and lay paralyzed on her bed until team members came and prayed for her. We believed this message was about the disunity of the church in the town—the lack of dovetail joints was the need for peace and reconciliation; the planks were the churches; the crash was areas of conflict.

Gathering the data from these unorthodox sources, we began to take action—as a team. We reconciled with one another; we fasted and prayed for the community; and we publicly addressed the disunity between the churches. In the days that followed, it was as if the natural were confirming the events in the supernatural—the rain and wind suddenly stopped, the sun peeked out from the clouds, the storm ceased (this after five weeks of unceasing foul weather), and the mission took off.

Faith Beyond Me

I remember talking with a man who was part of a cult that believed Jesus was the result of an alien coming to earth and having relations with Mary. Shocked, I spouted, "And how is it that you've come to believe such a thing?" In calm confidence, he returned, "By faith, I just have the faith to believe that it is true."

This is not the kind of faith upon which we rest. Our faith relies on substantiated proof that the God of the universe is regularly touching the life of humanity, in practical and meaningful ways, demonstrating that He is present with us.

Recalling the fourth year of our trek (summer and fall 1998), Russ had felt all along that part of his call was to see a unique Canadian expression of worship that would bring the whole Church together on the streets, not just through the Bandwagon, but also through the more broad-reaching, March For Jesus (MFJ). The MFJ board members agreed to go ahead with a national album with Russ as composer, and he had been trying to settle recording details as the Bandwagon continued with stops in Lindsay, Peterborough, Hamilton. But details were elusive and communications with the board coast-to-coast were challenging. Confusion, lost bookings and musicians, lack of time were a threat to hope, but we kept walking.

The town of Uxbridge, our most precious Ontario family, was our last stop before we were to cross into French Canada. After Uxbridge, we were off like nervous youths leaving home for the first time, this new frontier had us completely disoriented—in Québec we had no connections; the French language would be a challenge; and, with the regular Upstream work, time for recording would be difficult—but God seemed strangely in control. This musical baby was also going to be born in the right place at the right time.

Miracle #1: the only Québec community Upstream had been invited to, Morin Heights, Québec, Canada, just happened to have a world class recording studio where Celine Dion and Shania Twain completed albums. Miracle #2: this busy studio was available the week we arrived. Miracle #3: a talented group of French musicians were willing to translate and record so that the album could be in both of the nation's official languages.

This should have kept us optimistic, but when we arrived in Morin Heights and discovered we had no engineer and that the finances had suddenly fallen through just as the producer was arriving from England, we panicked. We questioned ourselves frantically and leapt into desperate prayers for God's mercy. "Help, God!" And He did. Unanticipated favor was given to us by the manager of the studio who allowed us to begin recording for free and led us to one of their top-notch engineers—who was also miraculously available that week.

Leading by the Still Waters

But we still needed the finances, tens of thousands of disconcerting dollars, and this I was nervously preparing myself to explain to our British producer, Steve, as I picked him up at his hotel. While Steve gulped down the last of his breakfast, he told me about the dream he had weeks before in England. "I was viewing the most beautiful scenery full of vibrant colors on sloping hills surrounding a shimmering lake…" he began. "As I watched silently, a leaf floated down onto the water and began to make ripples that kept going and going. The leaf eventually disappeared, but its impression remained on the surface of the water with a sense of peace."

Because the scene seemed familiar, he said he got up and poured through his nature books, and then finally woke his wife with a sense of urgency to express, and perhaps find meaning for, his dream. Even in her groggy state, she was suddenly aware, "Didn't someone in Canada tell us of something similar, of a leaf falling onto the water?" I interrupted, "I was the one who told your wife about that vision when you were last in Canada. A native woman had seen the leaf from the

Canadian flag fall on the Thompson and Fraser Rivers—native people dressed in their regalia were drinking from the rivers and were suddenly clothed in the white. Her sense was that the leaf, representing God's healing power, would bring healing to the nations." (See Revelation 22.)

I didn't know how it all fit together, but it seemed the appropriate time to tell Steve, "We don't yet have any of the funds for the project." "Hmmm," was his only response as we headed to the studio. While we toured the building, Steve peered out the window and gasped. We thought because of the beautiful scenery, full of vibrant colors on sloping hills surrounding a shimmering lake…whoa…it was the place in his dream! "The leaf," he said with sudden realization, "was the same as the leaf on the Canadian flag!" He ran to phone his wife. "We are in the place of my dream—God wants this project to go ahead, but the money is being held back. Pray!" In answer to prayer, by noon that day, all of the finances were in place (thanks to Justyn and Joy who interceded practically) and the project was on its way.

No Mind has Conceived

> *However, as it is written: 'No mind has seen, no ear has heard, no mind has conceived what God has prepared for those who love Him'—but God has revealed it to us by His Spirit. The Spirit searches all things, even the deep things of God* (1 Corinthians 2:9-10).

For Upstream's national journey, so many of the provisions and directions have been questionable and so, at strategic spots God put up street signs to assure us, "This is me! In my love and compassion, I am providing for you."

The spring of '97 brought us to the town where Jackie, an officer in the Salvation Army, lived. She was energetic and active and was stirring up as many Jesus-centered activities as possible in her quiet little town. One day, as Jackie sat in her home to pray for the needs of

Upstream, she suddenly got a vision of a man in the community giving Justyn a check for $2,000.

Rejoicing, she went to Justyn and inquired, "Have you received a check for $2,000 recently?" Puzzled, he responded, "No I haven't. Why?" Jackie just replied, "Oh we'll wait and see." The following day, the businessman who owned the parking lot where the Bandwagon was parked called Justyn into his office and wrote a check...for $2,000. Justyn blurted, "So, did you talk to Jackie?" The man looked up, bewildered, "No, I don't know any Jackie. Why?" Justyn hurried to Jackie's place for her to confirm, "Yes, this is the same man I had seen in my vision."

Sometimes God's direction is also protective. An organizing committee in one town was frantic—they had been battling for weeks to secure a prime piece of mall parking lot for the Bandwagon, but at the last minute, access was denied. Quickly but reluctantly, they booked the Armories facility at the other end of the city, conceding that they had to have somewhere to put us. The new site was less than ideal—it was hidden, not on a major road, not a desirable location—but it seemed to be God's divine provision.

After only two days of public presentations on this less than likely spot, we understood why—a freak weather system came through the area and a mini tornado bizarrely touched down right in the center of the city. Where? In the mall parking lot where the Bandwagon was originally scheduled to set up. The evening news showed damage-strewn streets, specifically lingering on the disquieting image of a semi-trailer truck that had been violently torn apart by the twister. God was taking care of us. Not only that, but because the Armories was a government property, not even the police had jurisdiction to shut us down.

Holy Fire

It is God who goes before us and sets about doing the work that He has called us to join with Him in. This is God, Lord of the Universe with whom we partner in honor and fear.

In another quiet, very religious community, a woman had been secretly, fervently praying for one of the local churches that was mixing the worship of spirits, other than the Spirit of God, with their Christian liturgy. Though she didn't know all of the church's activities, she was simply praying that whatever was not of God He would burn it up. She told no one of her prayers.

Shortly after arriving in town, the Upstream team set off to pray God's blessing on the local churches—two of our team specifically walked around that very church and felt prompted to pray, too, that the Lord would deal with the things that were not of Him. Shockingly, late that night, the church burned to the ground. The entire community grieved the loss. Some even suggested, "Could this have happened because of that 'cult group' (Upstream) up the street?"

The following evening in the Bandwagon, I sat praying with the woman, unaware of her previous prayers and her connection to the burned church. As I prayed, I had an strong impression in my mind, "Jeremiah 44" and so I turned to the passage and read aloud, *"They provoked me to anger by burning incense and by worshiping other gods that neither they nor you nor their fathers ever knew"* (Jeremiah 44:3). And, *"He* [the king of Babylon] *will set fire to the temples of the gods of Egypt; he will burn their temples and take their gods captive"* (Jeremiah 43:12). She began to weep, bursting with the cry, "Please have mercy Lord!" Her compassionate prayers had been for God's intervention to restore this fellowship to Him, but she had never intended for it to manifest itself in such an alarming way in the physical realm.

It was evident, though, in that town of many religions, that people were already confused about which god was the true God. How much more confusing was it to have a church proclaiming the true God, but amalgamating that truth with untruth? Could this have been God's unmistakable intervention? For us, this striking demonstration of God's jealousy for His Church was sobering and frightening.

Seeing in the Unseen

Obedience—the Prayer of Healing

In God's mercy, He also demonstrated His power in healing. Of course, our fake miracle man, Mike, had rattled the team, but we had continued to pray for healings even in the midst of our disillusionment. On the same evening of Mike's bogus miracle, a dynamic young couple had quietly shared with us their desperate grief about being unable to conceive a child after many years of marriage. Some of the team prayed with the wife for healing for her womb and for God's blessing of a child. Approximately nine months later, she gave birth to her first child.

During our very first summer, Bob, who was helping drive the truck for us, was suffering with an undetermined malady that left him in continuous pain. He was a gentle man with the demeanor of Eeyore (you know, Winnie the Pooh's donkey friend). "Oh it's okay," he'd say in the same slow, despondent tone, "I'll be all right." Daily he would trudge around the Bandwagon with agonizing steps, pausing to muster the strength to simply go up a stair.

At a church service one evening, visiting speakers invited people who needed healing to come forward for prayer. Hesitantly, Bob went and submitted his ailing body to their strong, authoritative prayers. Unfortunately, as he started to lumber back to his seat, it was evident that nothing had happened. The service ended but a determined Upstream member asserted, "I think we need to pray again for our friend." The team, together with the speakers, joined to pray again and immediately their prayers were answered. Bob, who had fallen to the floor as they prayed, now effortlessly stood up—he had been completely healed! Our gentle Bob who was Eeyore was miraculously transformed into a Tigger (you know, Pooh's obnoxious tiger buddy), with the same distinctive laugh in his talk and jovial bounce to his step—it was a full-fledged miracle!

On another evening in at the Bandwagon, Danny, a friendly 15-year-old local stood with Nate and Kathleen and watched as the team prayed for Christie, one of our members. A sudden yelp from the crowd encircling her indicated that their prayers had been answered and prompted Danny to blurt, "What're they doin'?" Nate and Kathleen looked at one another and explained, "They're praying for Christie's leg—she's not been able to walk on it all night and it looks like God has healed her."

A silent pause groped the air. "Would God do that for me too?" Danny queried. "My leg has been wrecked all year and I've not been able to do any sports." "Sure. Can we pray for it now?" He agreed and the two began to lift Danny's injury in prayer. When they finished, Danny started to rotate his leg, "Hey, it feels better!" Puzzled and shocked he stammered, "Th-thanks." No doubt he wasn't quite certain about it all, but the God he didn't yet know had obviously touched him with physical healing.

Setting Captives Free

And we have witnessed, God brings spiritual healing. In another town the local United Church pastor and I sat in prayer for a distressed middle-aged woman who was battling many disturbing thoughts, experiences, and dreams. In our differing, but congruent styles, John and I prayed through the terrible pain of the woman's childhood and then for her release from the spiritual powers that were oppressing her. As we took authority over any contrary spirits, she began to quiver and out of her mouth came the disturbing declaration, "No, she's my Mary!" With even greater determination and boldness we again ordered the spirit to be gone and for it not to speak or manifest itself through her body. There was a shudder and a sudden quiet calm as she was released.

What God consistently demonstrates is that the miraculous is simply His gift of compassion for our desperate and broken world and is a tool with which He sets the captives free, heals the broken and brings His Kingdom into our midst here on earth. What the miraculous is *not*, is food to satisfy our appetite for the experiential. As a wise teacher once told me, "If we seek after too much of the experiential, we will get fanaticism and if we ignore the experiential, we will get unbelief." Leaning on God for understanding, listening, testing, walking in obedience—these offer a safe path for reckless humanity to navigate in God's realm of the unseen.

Chapter 14

The Gift of Our Diversity

The nation of Canada is a place of cultural diversity as immense as its land mass; a place of divisions as plentiful as its accumulation of Tim Horton doughnut shops. The scars of prejudice and the undercurrents of animosity are the souvenirs of our endeavor to assemble this patchwork of provinces. The mosaic of Canada has been all the blessing and all the pain of attempting to establish many nations, tribes, and tongues in one place. Perhaps it was actually meant to be a little taste of Heaven.

Providentially, our histories collide. It seems to be one of the ways that God has been binding our cultures together. It was a French Jesuit missionary, Father Jean de Brébeuf, who first brought the Gospel to the native people through song in the Huron language in 1626.

> "Twas in the moon of wintertime when all the birds had fled,
> The Mighty Gichi Manitou sent angel choirs instead.
> When all at once the stars grew dim and wandering

hunters heard the hymn,
'Jesus your king is born, Jesus is born. In excelsis gloria.'"

Brébeuf died with the Huron people, refusing to leave when the Iroquois attacked and slaughtered the Huron nation.

In Montréal, late in 1998, we watched the same histories collide again. Marianne, a godly native woman from British Columbia was attending a national prayer conference with us. A local French Canadian missionary, Pierre, began to pray for Marianne on the final day and as he did, he began to pray in tongues. Marianne looked up in surprise. "Do you know what you are saying?" "No," Pierre responded. "I was just speaking in tongues." "You were just speaking in perfect 'Carrier,' my native tongue," she uttered. "You said, 'The Lord has opened the way, now go, and take the nation.'"

As One in His Hand

Early in our journey, the Ezekiel 37 passage began to speak to me in a powerful way. I had been especially moved by the segment when Ezekiel was commanded to take two sticks and join them together as one in his hand. *"The Lord said, 'I am going to take the stick of Joseph...and of the Israelite tribes associated with him, and join it to Judah's stick, making them a single stick of wood and they will become one in my hand...They will be my people and I will be their God'"* (Ezekiel 37:19b, 23b).

My spirit suddenly leapt at the possibility that God could do for Canada what He had promised to do for Israel (God's first nation)—that He could take Canada's First Nations and raise them up, dry bones and all, as a mighty army; that He would take the stick of the First Nations and the stick of the Second Nations (all of the other nations that settled here), and make them one in His hand. I sensed that this would not necessarily be a political unity; it would rather be a unity of the heart with Jesus on the throne as King.

The Gift of Our Diversity

First hand, I have been painfully aware of our nation's dilemma, as the divisions have resided in my extended family since before I was born. How much more peculiar can you get than my Japanese/German descent? My German mother, in her outspoken and gregarious manner, struggled to measure up to the expectations of her quiet, but influential, Japanese mother-in-law. My Japanese father was not given approval by his German father-in-law until the day my strong-minded grandfather died.

As a kid, I was aware of prejudice in every corner of my world. I knew I didn't belong to the German side of my heritage, because I looked too Japanese. I never laid claim to my Japanese birthright because of the shame my father always felt about being a Japanese man in post-war Canada (for him as a child, there was so much bad press, dad did everything he could to deny his Japanese heritage, including altering his prominent teeth and distinctive eyes which were grossly caricatured by the media). As a result, I didn't inherit anything of the Japanese culture. Where in the world did I belong?

It didn't hit me until we were halfway across the country—I had always felt like an orphan in my own land. Never had I perceived that I was a real Canadian, and yet I am third and fourth generation Canadian, I have never known another culture. During a Christmas service at a native church in Winnipeg, the whole thing welled up and overwhelmed me. I had been speaking about Jesus' desire to bring hope and reconciliation to Canada, but I was being personally impacted. Inviting Amy, a native woman, to come forward, I asked if she would be willing to adopt me—as though I were being adopted by my nation—as her daughter. She agreed, the pastor anointed us with oil and prayed that this act would be symbolic of God binding the stick of the First Nations and the stick of the Second Nations as one in His hand.

Weaving Our Histories

On the day that we met up with an exceptional Québecker by the name of Jean-Claude, our national pilgrimage again intersected with history. We had heard Jean-Claude share, in French, at a conference and we had cornered him with our questions about the French culture. As we expressed our heart for the nation, he suddenly said, "You know, I had an interesting experience while I was in Winnipeg. A native woman adopted me because I, as a French Canadian, felt like an orphan in my own country." This stranger, now a brother, had been spiritually adopted by the same spiritual mom, Amy, almost a year after I had.

Encouragement from God has consistently appeared in the direction of His love for our diversity. The pain of this diversity is thankfully compensated for by its blessing. As representatives of the many cultures of the world the "every nation tribe language people fearing God and giving Him glory" phenomenon could begin here. To the French and to the native, to the English and Indian, to the Ukrainian and Chinese, to the Italian and African—God is saying, "For my sake, go and take the nation."

Our biggest challenge: loving one another.

The French Connection

> The Almighty in His infinite wisdom did not see fit to create Frenchmen in the image of Englishmen.
>
> —Sir Winston Churchill

One of the few national dynamics that we had anticipated as an enormous challenge was the French-English relationship. As we slid into Québec in late fall 1998, James, one of our team, saw a profound picture. In it, the red from the Canadian flag began to pour out—alongside it, the blue of the Québec flag began to pour out and the mix of the two became visibly one color, purple. James sensed that the purple (royalty) was symbolic of Jesus taking His place as King over the nation of Canada, and it seemed to say, "Unity under Jesus will bring healing to the Canada/Québec issue."

And healing has been a necessary factor. The people of Québec are gentle and sensitive with an enormous heart of love, but the devastating history of oppression by the English has left them embittered. The battle fought in Canada was the continuation of centuries of war between the French and English, waged in strategic spots around the world; but here, French and English were brought into a pact of national union. Though Canada is decidedly French and English in its national languages, the French were rarely permitted to speak their language and the nation's activities continued predominantly in English for generations. But recently the "Quiet Revolution" has amplified the voice of the French Canadian once again and the French culture has been regaining prominence.

The Lord has fashioned a fascinating gate in the fence around this two-culture struggle—our national anthem. It was originally a French hymn that was eventually adopted as the Canadian national anthem and translated to the current Canada-friendly version. But in the original French, it speaks of a victor, a cross, a crown of victory…could this be Jesus, the victor, with the power of the Cross and the emblem of a crown of thorns? Could it be we once believed that, with Jesus as Lord over our nation, there could be victory for the sake of our unity and peace as James' vision of purple suggests?

Our Part

Unmistakably, the effort has only just begun. Even in the name of Jesus, the church has anchored itself to political platforms and inadvertently batted at our French brothers, mistaking a political reconciliation with God's reconciliation. Aware of our own ineptness to reach the people of French Canada, we pressed Jean-Claude, "So, what do we do to reach the people of Québec?" His response was simple, "Just love them…if they see your love, they will open their hearts to you."

Our projects in Québec came on the heels of several months of orientating ourselves to this new culture. We needed to revise our Bandwagon program—too many of our messages from the three previous years could be misunderstood as having political overtones. We concluded that we would simply express the love of God and salvation through Jesus, the same conclusion the apostle Paul came to: *"For I resolved to know nothing while I was with you except Jesus Christ and him crucified"* (1Corinthians 2:2).

Our efforts to speak in French and to nurture relationship became our language of love, though frequent miscommunications forced us to also make our own repentance primary. On the eve before the public launch of the MFJ album, misunderstandings, perceived injury, and confusion were unleashed between us and our French counterparts—as though the historical wars were discharging their fury on this very moment. But it was nothing that our immediate repentance couldn't redeem. By the celebrated night, we were peacefully restored to one another in joy and passionate fellowship—the atmosphere in the auditorium was electric as, united, we worshiped one Lord in our two languages.

A New Education

In Québec our greatest opportunities to share the Gospel were in the public schools. As the province was departing, en masse from their cultural faith, the Catholic Church (the Quiet Revolution), all sorts of religious experimentation was being embraced, including the expression of the "Protestant Gospel." Unlike anywhere else in the nation, we were able to talk about Jesus in classrooms, at assemblies, and one-on-one with students and teachers. In one Montréal high school class, a Christian English teacher had invited us to present our entire message to her class.

The discussion afterward was intended to give the French students practice speaking English, but it erupted into a challenge of belief—some shot out that they didn't need to believe in God; some accused us of being a cult; some thought we were trying to brainwash them; one teacher declared it was a ridiculous message. The silent student segment came to us afterward—fear had kept them from sharing their appreciation publicly—but they eagerly confessed, "Our school really needs the love of God. We're sorry that the other students were so unkind to you." Without hesitation they accepted our invitation to pray for Jesus and His love to invade their school. The Christian teachers were thrilled—they sensed the doors were now open for conversations about Jesus with the students (even the irate ones).

A Faulty Unity

The message of unity that so strongly dominated our presentations in the rest of Canada suddenly seemed irreverent on this sensitive soil. It was here we discovered that an overemphasis on national unity can actually derail the purposes of God. Jesus said, *"Do not suppose that I have come to bring peace to the earth, I did not come to bring peace, but a sword"* (Matt. 10:34). Jesus was aware that peace by the world's understanding and by the world's methods would never bring God's peace.

By example, many of the unity efforts in Canada's history have had damaging consequences. The building of the Canadian railway in the 1880s was pushed ahead in a desperate effort to maintain sovereignty and unity across the vast, sparsely populated country. The death of hundreds of the 6,000 Chinese workers testifies to the great cost of this endeavor. (My Japanese grandfather worked with them setting the dynamite for blasting the rock—the job with the highest mortality rate—he was one of the few to survive.)

Additionally, as federal funds were depleting the government was faced with choosing to uphold the native treaties (feeding them in their season of famine) or to build the railroad (the steel link to unity)—they chose the latter. Thousands of aboriginal people were left starving and dying.

Decades later Canada faced yet another decision of unity versus compassion. A shipload of Jews, who had escaped the Nazi invasion of Europe during World War II, laid their final request for asylum before the Canadian government. Though it concurred with public policy, tensions were growing between the dissenters and the consenters and a resulting rift was widening between the French and English. The final decision was to reject the request on the basis of the need to maintain French and English unity.

The ship, the St. Louis, was forced to return to Europe where Hitler released orders to begin the "Final Solution"—the extermination of the Jews. Shortly following the St. Louis' arrival in Europe, many of the Jews were taken into the Nazi concentration camps and a significant number were put to death.

How Diversity Brings Unity

Anyone who loves his father or mother more than me is not worthy of me; anyone who loves his son or daughter more than me is not worthy of me; and anyone who does not take his cross and follow me is not worthy of me. Whoever finds his life will lose it, and whoever loses his life for my sake will find it.... And if anyone gives a cup of cold water to one of these little ones because he is my disciple, I tell you the truth; he will certainly not lose his reward (Matthew 10:37-39,42).

Relinquishing our right to our heritage (loving Jesus more than our parents); relinquishing our right to pass on our heritage (loving Jesus more than our children); dying to ourselves (taking up our cross); offering grace to those we consider the least (a cup of cold water to one of the little ones)—this is how to give birth to the unity and peace that God speaks of. Holding on too tightly to the sanctity of our culture, could cause it to become our god.

The Gift of Our Diversity

Curiously, the demands that our cultural diversity places on our comfort zones is what seems to push us out of them. Looking as an example at our team of ambassadors who set off across the nation; we were a motley assortment of the nation's ethnicity. Overcoming the aggravating challenge of daily living at peace with our differences is the hammer that forges understanding. Written into the histories of struggle for these cultures to embrace one another is the blessed prospect that God's love might prevail.

CHAPTER 15

In Hot Water—Baptism and Other Suspicious Activities

As you might expect, there were times in the journey when our activities posed an amount of threat to some communities, as well as to some churches. The hot topics for the churches—worship styles, speaking in tongues, communion, baptism. For communities, our strange theatre and its activities was enough to send up red flags. Our best intentions weren't going to be enough, we needed the direction and protection of the Lord, and lots of discernment.

Snuggled at the feet of the Laurentien Mountains of Québec in a snowy backyard lot, our motorhome was thankfully pumping furnace heat as I peered out the windows. I could hear Russ' irritated voice echoing from somewhere outside, but I was unable to determine from where and why. Uh, there's a familiar sound, the "Chip, chip, chip" of Russ' hatchet on the ice under the motorhome. Why? To move the motorhome for its weekly sewage dump, Russ had to spend laborious hours chipping the stabilizer legs out of the ice. Today, he had also slid full-body under the rig and was unable to get footing to slither out of the slushy, slippery ice-muck. Ah, winter again!

Who Are You?

In this quiet village in French Canada, most of the team had settled into rental homes and we were meeting daily to practice our French and to develop new, creative methods of communication for this radically different culture and language. Little did we know the stir that we were causing.

Unbeknownst to us, this unassuming mountain village, Morin Heights, had been the hideout for several questionable cults over the years—the latest, the "Solar Temple" had terminated its existence through a mass suicide just a few years previous. The small population of locals were suspicious of our group, "You've come from where and do what? Do your parents know?" The chatter of good ol' boys at the diner up the hill, would suddenly quiet when any of us walked in. For certain we "looked" questionable. We were young and overly enthusiastic; living a communal lifestyle; had decrepit vehicles and not much money; and presented a seemingly "new" message about God. People remained aloof and cautious.

On the day of our departure from the area (spring 1999), a van load of team members were inexplicably stopped by the police—they were looking for members of a reported cult. As we arrived in our new locale, across the river from Ottawa, Justyn received a call from a friend in the Vancouver police department: "Justyn, I received a call from the Ottawa police. They were alerted by the Québec police that there was a cult group headed into their area and wanted information about the group 'Upstream.' I let them know that that you were a well grounded group of Christians—amazing that I would be the one to receive the call. God is sure taking care of you guys!"

Hot Water

For just such reasons, our team chose to deliberately steer clear of any extreme or controversial activities and stick to preaching the Word. Unfortunately, another piece of Justyn's visionary puzzle was

In Hot Water—Baptism and Other Suspicious Activities

that he felt we could not step away from one controversial mandate—to baptize. Jesus had commissioned, *"...make disciples of all nations, **baptizing** them in the name of the Father and of the Son and of the Holy Spirit..."* (Matt. 28:19)—not just discipleship, but also baptism. God confirmed this detail by making the first donation to our project a baptismal tank in the form of a hot tub.

But what of the centuries of controversy we were about to enter? Is it a graduation or an initiation? As a child or as an adult? Sprinkled, poured, or immersed? In a church? A river? After planned baptismal classes or spontaneous?

The argument is no better expressed than the day a Scottish theologian walked into a meeting, clearly agitated by a recent conversation he had had with an English theologian. They had been peacefully working together on a theological commentary of the Gospels, but upheaval arose as they reached the topic of "how" Jesus was baptized. Suddenly, the immersion tradition of the Scot, a Baptist, came crashing against the pouring tradition of the Brit, an Anglican. The Scot, irate that the Anglican's evidence of Jesus' pouring had come from an old and famous painting, bellowed, "Can you believe it? [He] gets his theology from pic-chur-r-res!"

Coming Clean

Oblivious to the controversy, people have responded willingly to being baptized. In Lumby, British Columbia (September 1996), a small town riddled with drug and alcohol abuse, the Bandwagon had been planted across from the local pub and hungry locals crowded in to hear our presentation of hope. Some of them, visibly drunk, would yell and heckle as the program progressed ("Hey, would ya stop the talkin', I wanna hear more music!"), but the message was, nonetheless, powerfully touching hearts.

On the last evening a middle aged man sat in the audience, watching as his family lined up to be baptized—he finally lumbered forward to talk to Justyn. "See this scar?" He pulled up his shirt exposing an enormous gash on his back containing a hidden souvenir of shrapnel. "I did military service and this is what I got—I've been angry and bitter with God ever since," he said. "I've made life in my household hell…" he trailed off, overcome by emotions and conviction. "If my family is finding peace with God, then so can I." He was baptized then and there—a whole family saved.

One Baptism

Queries and concerns persist: "How do you baptize in an interchurch situation?" I am no expert in the debate, but my upbringing as the daughter of a Baptist pastor and an old-order-Mennonite-turned-Pentecostal-turned-Baptist mom does, though, lead me into the chaos of it all. There is a certain fogginess in doctrine and practice that has clouded this one radical act. Christians have not been a particularly powerful force in North America in past few decades—perhaps this one radical act, done publicly, could produce more radical disciples. A raised hand or coming forward is one thing, but how much more impact is baptism on the street of your own community, in front of those who know you and see you in everyday life?

But who is to do it? Local pastors and priests? The visiting evangelists? Which style? How do you ensure that the commitment is real? What if they've already been baptized? We've been through the full gamut of questions; but person by person, as they are responding to Jesus, we have trusted God to care for the details.

We faced the dilemma head-on as a young woman, teary-eyed and intent on being baptized, approached me one evening. The complications? She had just begun attending a Catholic Church, so in respect for the pouring tradition of her church, having never been baptized as a child, and because of a recent surgery, she didn't want to be immersed. I called over the local Baptist pastor and explained the situation. He looked at the ground long and hard before responding. "My deacons have entered discussions this week about whether we'd accept someone not baptized by immersion—there were no final conclusions…but… you know…" he grinned. "I see no reason why this woman should not be baptized now and in this way." So he poured over her head the symbol of reconciliation: between this woman and her Lord; between the divisions in the church.

Like apostle Paul, we did not baptize, except only a few people. Initially we did some baptizing, but we found it better if the local pastors did it according to their various traditions. In this way, the pastors and their fellowships could take responsibility for the people they baptized and, quite frankly, we saw some amazing things happen when the pastors came together to baptize.

Nelson, British Columbia (October 1996), a town not just of many denominations but of many religions, the Church of Christ needed to make a united stand. They were already meeting regularly for interchurch prayer and it was apparent, consequently, that God was beginning do a powerful work in the town. Many people were taking the step to be baptized publicly in our Bandwagon hot tub, but the "pastor" who was doing most of it was Dave, the Salvation Army captain (considered a mission and not a church, the Salvation Army, as a fellowship, doesn't baptize). While baptizing the last candidate, this realization suddenly dawned on Dave and he declared, "You know, I've never been baptized," and turning to the non-denominational pastor and the Presbyterian minister, inquired, "Would you two do the honor?" In an instant all three were in the tub and Dave was baptized by his brothers. Throughout the surrounding crowd, eyes were suddenly damp as we recognized this demonstration of God drawing His Church together.

It has not always been so easy.

Washing One Another's Feet

Getting back to Québec—the Evangelical church here is relatively young, having grown up during the Quiet Revolution over the last couple of decades. The province sits as one of North America's least evangelized people groups (less than 0.5% Evangelical Christian), but never have we witnessed such a hunger to hear the Gospel; never has the Bandwagon been bursting with such power in celebration. The passion and the freedom of the French people are unequaled anywhere else in Canada.

Our treading sensitively (perhaps a bit fearfully) with these communities, logically spilled over into the area of baptism as well. Here in Québec, we saw that there was so much newness and learning and jostling in these young churches, the issue of baptism seemed poised to introduce unnecessary added confusion, especially since many had Catholic roots and had been baptized as infants. Therefore, for the first time since we set out, we avoided the subject during the Outaouais project (including Hull, Aylmer and Gatineau) as well as in the subsequent one in the Montréal suburb of Laval.

But our final Québec project was in Cowansville, and here the churches were well established and had already worked together in public settings—it seemed beneficial, even logical, to open up the tank. Sure enough, a steady stream of seekers from off the street poured into the Bandwagon, responding with joy to Jesus and visibly eager to be baptized. We encouraged the local pastors to do the baptizing and, due to the tradition of those particular clergymen, all were immersed. Everything seemed peaceful until a couple of days into the project when one pastor, arriving late in the program, witnessed several of his parishioners—those who had been baptized as children—being baptized again and this time by immersion. A pained complaint was expressed in his single agitated challenge, "Is this 'one baptism'?"

Justyn called an immediate meeting of all the pastors, "Please, let us not allow this issue to divide us," he pleaded. The collection of clergy sat in somber silence as Justyn shared, encouraging the pastors to embrace this new thing (baptizing together) and exhorting them to respond in peace. The group parted after prayer and we cautiously

In Hot Water—Baptism and Other Suspicious Activities

carried on with another Bandwagon evening, this time closing the baptismal tank so as to not push the issue.

But the final night of the project seemed different—the crowds that packed the bleachers and jammed the doorways, were charged with exuberant response—so we decided to open the tank again, this time witnessing the miracle of Jesus' reconciled Bride. For me a single image, among the numerous baptisms that took place that night, lingers. A charismatic pastor, standing waist-deep in the water, is immersing a young woman. And there, sitting with pant legs rolled up and feet dangling in the water, is that concerned pastor, washing the feet of one of his congregation (baptized as a child, now making an adult commitment). Could this be what Jesus meant when he said, *"A person who has had a bath needs only to wash his feet; his whole body is clean…"* (John 13:10a)?

The humility and gracious acceptance those pastors offered one another is a tangible example of how Jesus has called us to wash one another's feet—it's a distinct challenge for the church to lay down our differences and trust God to deal with the details. In this way, we can dare to be radical with the Gospel—when we seek to be obedient to Him, the things that are of Him will come to the surface, the things that are not will fall away.

CHAPTER 16

I'm the Farmer Now— From Seed to Sowing

And then there were "those days" when our work in the nation looked like anything but a harvest. Those times when *"The harvest is plentiful…"* seemed to be calloused words of taunt, enhancing feelings of failure. Those times and places of barrenness had the same ominous theme—plowing. We had distinctly set off on our vagabond journey to harvest, but plowing seemed to be our main vocation—the frequency of plow-soliciting locations was as predictable as it was disheartening.

A kindhearted woman cornered Justyn after a particularly unfruitful evening in the Bandwagon. "I believe the Lord is telling me that you are being called to plow. That's why you aren't seeing a harvest right now," the woman soothed. "Don't be discouraged." Justyn graciously thanked her for the "word", but as he walked toward Russ, he muttered sarcastically, "If I hear one more person say that we're plowing, I'll spit!"

So what does a team of harvesters do when they come to a place that's not been plowed or sown? Move on? If we don't do the plowing, who does? And doesn't the sower (see Matthew 13) just scatter seed? Do we even *need* to plow?

Conclusion? We're farmers, doing the work in God's fields. Every farmer knows that to see the harvest, he has to be part of the plowing, planting, watering, and cultivating—it goes with the territory. As traveling farmers, we needed to join in with the work that the field of each community required.

Behind the Plow

The success of Upstream's spring and early summer 1999 in Québec had us riding high as we lunged into the Maritime Provinces by the end of June. Because we had erroneously presumed that these provinces were just like the rest of English Canada, we were not adequately prepared for the greater conservatism, the slower pace of life, reserved response, and the disarming politeness. Perhaps not so threatening to most, but with our renegade methods—the brash music; adventurous, sometimes confrontational program; the request for public response; and the casual, off-the-cuff communication—we frequently managed to rock the Maritime boat.

Our first stop, Quispamsis, New Brunswick, was a riverside stretch of Saint John suburbia with an air of comfortable prosperity. The polite rejection of our invitations to the Bandwagon and the quickly closed doors caught us off guard. "I have everything I need. I am a good person and I believe in God. That's good enough," they declared and stayed their distance throughout the project. Hard ground.

Discouragement, disorientation, despondency had victoriously laid hold of our ranks and, for the first time in many months, we considered finishing our journey there. With the success of Québec, we had truthfully hoped that our work would now be a little less agonizing, a little more prolific. But here we again set to plowing—prayer, proclamation, and public worship. When our time was done, the responsibility to plant and to harvest was left for the locals to complete.

Sowing the Seed

From there we moved just an hour down the road to the tiny town of St. George, New Brunswick, a picturesque community hemmed in by the Bay of Fundy and perched high on a riverside ridge. There was little sign of life apart from the busy ice cream shop and the heritage health food store, but the miniscule town center suddenly bubbled alive in early July 1999, when the Bandwagon rigs overwhelmed the main street's only parking lot.

With little advertisement, the Bandwagon was bursting with attendees—people from the town, church-goers from all congregations came, enjoyed and returned on subsequent nights, complete with neighbors in tow. Considering such enthusiasm and receptivity, we were stunned by the lack of overt response to our message. "Maritimers are slow to respond," people justified, "just give them some time and they will."

Undeniably, for the group of interested students who regularly poked their heads in for the program, our hope-filled message took on a new urgency. On one muggy evening, just as Nathan was about to share his testimony, an ambulance rushed past, its siren silencing the sound of his voice. There at the street's end, imprisoned in flames and twisted metal, was a young teen, who was burning to death after rolling his truck. Tail-spinning in a vortex of grief, the students gathered at the accident's dreadful site while paramedics labored in vain to salvage their friend's broken body. In the days that followed, they returned to the Bandwagon one-by-one, desperately looking for answers and ultimately seeking any hope we had to offer. The seed was hitting the fertile ground of receptive hearts.

Scattering Abroad

Sowing is always one of the greatest unknowns—you never know what will, and will not, take root—but presumably, the more seed that goes out, the more potential success. For instance, Maurice, a local from Hull, Québec, (May 1999) stepped onto the porch of a gruff middle-aged French man to offer an invitation to the Bandwagon and to toss a seed. The man was deliberately abrasive as Maurice offered the invitation, stating right off that he wanted nothing to do with that "religious" stuff. In friendship, Maurice kept the conversation going and tossed out the comment, "Well then you wouldn't be wanting this book" (Maurice was holding the book, *I Am*—answering the question, "Is there a God?") "Now I wouldn't say that," the man rebutted and took the book...scattering seed.

> I'm the farmer now, not the soil
> Now that I've received
> I'll return the deed...
> Seeds of love, seeds of joy, seeds of peace
> Seeds of truth, seeds of grace will increase
> They will grow, they will know
> That His love has been shown to the last and
> the lost and the least
>
> (From "The Farmer Song" by Russ Rosen © 1995)

The Harvest

The end of July 1999 we set up the Bandwagon in Grand Bay, New Brunswick, just up river from Saint John—only a Dairy Queen and a couple of strip malls identified the existence of a town. An enthusiastic collection of local pastors and priests, loving this new experience in unity, headed their town's eager involvement in the Bandwagon. Maritimers were finally responding! After only a few days, many accepted God's gift of forgiveness through Jesus; others wanted prayer and still others were baptized. Hallelujah! The harvest!

In the crowd that came to the front one night, was Bill, a man from the previous town we were in, St. George. His concerned, determined, wife had dragged him to the Bandwagon when we were in their town, but he hadn't shown any signs of response. Then without a word he had headed off on a fishing trip. Little did his wife know that her slow-to-respond Maritimer was about to have two full days with nothing but the lap of the water and the swirl of his unceasing thoughts to process what he had heard. Bill reasoned through his life, "Something has to change," he finally concluded. When he returned home, Bill made a resolute declaration to his stunned wife, "We've got to go back to the Bandwagon. There are some things I need to get straightened out with God."

This time, as the invitation for response was offered, there was no hesitation from Bill—he sprang forward, with his whole family, to turn his life over to Jesus.

Working in the Field

Sometimes we've had the pleasure of joining in with what the Church of a community has already begun itself. In the sleepy riverside town of Lindsay, Ontario (July 1998), two small church fellowships were hard at work, preparing the field of the their town for the planting of the Kingdom of God. The one was spending most its energies plowing, through: faithful intercession; joint worship events; and, the support for other fellowships. The other was scattering seed (going to their neighbors' doors) with a boldness that put we Upstreamers to shame. And the rest of the churches were conscientiously doing the work of maintaining a firm grounding in the Word of God and praying for the salvation of their town.

The water of Holy Spirit-empowered relationship was poured out as we arrived in town and joined with the churches to publicly proclaim the Gospel. Together, in the park on main street, we presented a worship concert in the gazebo. Together, at the town's Riverfest event, we sang and declared the Truth from the main stage. Together we knocked on doors and introduced people to God. Together we stood in the Bandwagon. The reception in that town was enormous—nearly every evening many people took the plunge in the baptismal tank. We had come to do the harvesting, but God had installed our venue as the threshing floor—the place for processing the harvest.

We discovered that the simple act of desperate people coming together to seek God for His mercy, even in an extended season of spiritual drought, initiates the work that tills up the spiritual soil of a place. As God affirmed:

> *...if my people, who are called by my name, will humble themselves and pray and seek my face and turn from their wicked ways, then will I hear from heaven and will forgive their sin and will heal their land* (2 Chronicles 7:14).

Flood With Your Tide

Truro, our next stop on the east coast, sits unassumingly along the banks of its main tourist attraction, the Tidal Bore—a unique natural phenomenon where the force of the tide reverses the flow of the sea bound river, overwhelming its muddy basin with a fresh flood of ocean water. The locals affectionately call it the Total Bore—it's how they seemed to feel about their lot in life. At the onset of this town's history, the forefathers hoped it would become a booming metropolis of commerce and activity, but it never happened. Today, even the hordes of churches (in one downtown area there are eight within just two city blocks) are struggling to bolster the town's hopefulness, as people tumble into sinful lifestyles. But God was at His work here, giving birth to something new.

The freshly-elected mayor was a man of radical conviction. He had declared in his victory speech that it was God who had put him in office and no matter what the cost he would fully pursue God's purposes for the city. He greeted people at the entrance to the Bandwagon every night and joyfully supported all of our activities. On our final evening, he stood to give his own testimony: "This Jesus that I am speaking of is the only hope for Truro. Please respond by turning your life back to God." He also quietly confided to us, "I know that a lot of what I say publicly may mean the end of my political career, but it's worth the risk, don't you think?"

Russ wrote a song for Truro that declared God's plans for the town:

> The riverbank reveals its silt,
> As the tide of life rolls out at will.
> The tidal bore rolls up the shore,
> The mercy of God is new once more.
> Mercy of God wash over me.
> My heart is stained, O please forgive.
> And all my desires, all of my pride,
> Cleanse with your river, flood with your tide.

(From: "Mercy of God" by Russ Rosen © 1999)

In the pub next door, our music team managed to echo these same truths. An invitation came from pub owners for our band to play in exchange for our use of their power and water. We were pleasantly surprised how "at home" our music was in this strange environment where couples danced, people socialized, and others although drunk, unwittingly and enthusiastically joined in the celebration of the love of God. We shouldn't have been so surprised—after all, Jesus was more at home among the everyday people, the drunks, the lonely, than He was with church people.

In the Bandwagon, people were alive with response, the whole town rose to take action. Many came for prayer, many turned their lives over to Jesus, and many were baptized. A new name for Truro? "Mercy of God."

I remembered years previous when Jackie Pullinger had boldly confronted Russ and I just as we were headed in to lead worship at a mission's conference. She had a disturbed look as she challenged, "Why are you doing this here?" I flushed with puzzled embarrassment, "What exactly do you mean?" She continued, "Everyone in here already knows this message, why don't you go to those who don't know it?" I questioned her again, "Do you really think we could do this out on the streets—with those who aren't Christians?" inwardly preparing for the consequences of her probable response. "Of course, they would love it!"

Now, after our pub and street performances—we understand.

More Workers

We left Truro by early September 1999 and descended to the red-sandy shores of Prince Edward Island—home of the young Lucy Maud Montgomery (*Anne of Green Gables*) and the establishment of the Confederation of Canada. Here, the glass pop bottle has royal position, banishing all other forms of canned or plastic bottled beverages from her domain (an effort to sustain her own small bottling industry). Here, a fictional literary figure named "Anne" has her own theme town and inspires the pilgrimage of many a Japanese tourist, some of whom will walk the several days journey from the airport to the revered "Anneland" in homage. Here, God was also at work.

An elderly woman in Charlottetown, was greeted at her door by Bruce, an Upstreamer, and his partner from the community. As they finished a brief conversation and prayer, Bruce asked the woman, "Would you be willing to confess that Jesus Christ is your Lord." She responded openly, "I believe in God, but I don't think I've ever done that. I guess I'd be willing." Bruce continued, "Would you like to do it right now?" "Well, yes I would," was the gentle, uninhibited answer. "I confess Jesus Christ is my Lord."

Bruce and his partner were thrilled by this quick and painless response, but what they didn't know was that groundwork had been going on well before their arrival. For years, this woman's son, a strong Christian, been talking to her about Jesus, but she had never responded. They had come at just the right time to see the plant sprout. This was a repeated theme in this city and we simply joined

I'm the Farmer Now— From Seed to Sowing

in on a harvest that previous generations of Christians had worked for in unity.

Very often we were simply the "more workers" needed for the harvest. In June 1998 in Hanover, a small former furniture boom town in rural southern Ontario, organizers managed to secure a sight for the Bandwagon right in the center of the downtown. Due to the decline of the furniture industry and other difficult economic dynamics, this town's face was painted with signs of financial adversity. Yet the air seemed fresh with hope as masses of people crowded our Solomon's Colonnade from the very first day. For a town of only 6,000, the enormous crowd seemed out of proportion—strong church interconnections were the blessed cause.

The town churches loved each another and had already been expressing that love to their community. There was no fear or apprehension among the unchurched and the Bandwagon was buzzing with excitement and anticipation as we presented the Gospel message to the crowds. Each evening people of all ages responded to Jesus and the reveling church stepped in to build relationships with their neighbors who became their brothers.

On the Threshing Floor

So, how do we deal with the harvest, those who are coming into a relationship with Jesus? Taking a look at Old Testament references to threshing floors (where the harvest was processed) makes the answer obvious. It is apparent that they were often treated as holy places—Jacob made sure he was buried by the threshing floor of Atad (see Genesis 50:10); Gideon meets the Lord at the threshing floor (see Judges 6:37); Ruth is blessed by Boaz on the threshing floor (see Ruth 3:2); God stops the plague on the Israelites at the threshing floor of Araunah (see 2 Samuel 24:16); the temple that Solomon builds was on that same threshing floor (2 Chronicles 3:1)—hey, Solomon's Colonnade was on a threshing floor!

The harvest is God's territory; it is not a commodity to be shuffled to this church or that, nor is it spoils from a battle won; it is meaningful relationship glued together by the love of God poured through His people. Christine, in Powell River, British Columbia (September 1995), an energetic middle-aged woman with natural mothering attributes, had become deeply involved with our mission in her town. So when Kim, a young single mom, was baptized, Christine took her own step and got together with Kim for regular Bible study and discipleship, making herself available for advice, prayer, friendship, affirmation, and direction. She was a signpost pointing the way to the Lord that they both were following.

Yet realistically, as careful as we might be, even if we fail to build a relationship with the new believer, they are positively safe in the hands of God himself. Take a look at the Ethiopian after Philip's input; the man was left on his own to walk out his faith (see Acts 8:26). And nearly 2,000 years later, the evidence of his adequacy to depend solely on the Lord is the present thriving Ethiopian Christian Church which traces its origin to that one man.

And truly there is an element of discipleship, which demands initiative not pampering. Arthur, a 70ish man in Swift Current, Saskatchewan, (August 1997) was raised in a nominal way in a mainline Christian Church—a living relationship with Jesus was evidently a new concept for him. He focused intently on the message each evening and returned to us each day to show how the Word of God was transforming his life. "I went to an old pastor of mine yesterday and asked forgiveness for the years of bitterness and unforgiveness toward him. I feel so free now. Thanks for pointing the way." When Jesus called His disciples, He just kept walking and they had to take the initiative to get in stride with Him, to keep walking with Him, to learn from Him.

Bananas Through Rungs

Conversely, as the Body of Christ (the Church), we have the blessed challenge before us to express the love of Jesus to those who don't yet know Him and to those who are new at knowing Him. We need to take care that we don't allow all of our time to be eaten up by those close to us and miss the opportunity to care for those outside our circle who need God's love.

Regrettably, we are sometimes like the following example. A friend of mine had just given birth to her first baby and recruited her sister, a Harvard graduate, to care for the infant so she and her husband could go out for the evening. Upon her arrival home three hours later, my friend, hearing the screaming child from the driveway, rushed into the house. She found her sister upstairs, helplessly standing beside the crib as the baby's wails continued. Mother quickly picked up the child and within seconds had calmed the distressed infant. My friend, concerned at how despairing the child had been, asked her sister how long the tot had been crying. "Essentially, since you left," she said confidently. "I tried feeding him bananas through the rungs of the crib, but he wouldn't take it." "Did you try picking him up?" asked the mother. The scholar's response: "Oh, you know, I never thought of that."

Personal contact requires an emotional commitment of us. The expression of God's love through us infringes on our lives. It prevents us from standing at a distance, feeding evangelism, doctrine, and discipleship clinically—like bananas through rungs. It demands that we allow the pain and despair of another to spew onto our Sunday best and provide the kind of care that enables these babes grow to maturity.

CHAPTER 17

The Young and the Rest

Children. Second class citizens in adult-dominated North America. It's no wonder we Upstreamers fell into the same trap as the disciples, minimizing the importance of their presence. And yet Jesus said, *"I tell you the truth, anyone who will not receive the kingdom of God like a little child will never enter it"* (Mark 10:15). It has been the youth and the children who have been most open to the Gospel. They know Truth when they hear it; they know love when they feel it. Coming to Jesus is based on the simple need for love and of responding to Truth. The young, even in the midst of their being silly and goofing around, open their hearts to the Word of God. This message that we treat with solemn seriousness—how can the young fully embrace its meaning and impact? Simply, they just can.

A young woman from the Northwest Territories explained to me how she found God. As a child, she had been invited by friends to Vacation Bible School at one of the churches in her town. On the afternoon the speaker gave the call to receive Jesus, she hadn't heard— she was actually in a conflict with the girl next to her and at that very moment, the other girl jabbed her in the ribs so hard, she began to cry. Seeing the weeping child, the speaker descended on the girl with ruthless determination. "Is Jesus touching your heart?" the evangelist gushed at the poor victim. In an instant she was being led in a prayer to accept Jesus and astonishingly, that decision has been rooted in her life since that day—she's now headed toward full-time ministry.

Josh, 13, and his buddy, Shawn (Aldergrove, 1995) were wheeling around the mall parking lot when the first of our painted trailers invaded their space. They hung around everyday for three weeks, developing friendships and getting a taste of the message. It was Russ who finally got down to business and asked Josh the question, "What do you want God to do for you?" Josh paused, still playing it cool. "Well…my sister is making our home life really angry and painful…" "Let's pray about that," Russ shot back. Together they brought this issue before God and then Russ asked, "Would you like to accept Jesus into your life?" Josh: "Yeah, I'd like that." A week later, Josh was also baptized.

Shawn's mother was dying of cancer, so the team rallied around him in prayer, taking the anguish of his family before their Heavenly Father and in just a matter of days, Shawn, too, gave his life over to Jesus. His mother died shortly afterward but Shawn and his family were grateful for our input into Shawn's life during those critical weeks.

Embracing the Young

I should have learned my lesson as director of a summer camp years previous, but I had developed a careless attitude regarding the youngest campers and God rebuked me, "Don't you know how important these young ones are? Their hearts are unclaimed ground; if they can know Me now, it will affect the rest of their lives."

September 1999 marked the beginning of the closing months of our cross-national adventure and we were becoming accustomed to the effortless pleasure of easy and numerous responses. But here in our new site, Summerside, Prince Edward Island, the response wasn't what we had expected—it was children. The disinterest of the adults of the community had us seriously distracted by our errant conclusion that our efforts were, once again, useless. Following our visit to the schools, dozens of young elementary students had eagerly poured to the Bandwagon—leaping to the stage, embarrassing us all with their crazy, irreverent dancing, galloping up and down the stairs, wandering in and out of the doorways—and then, willingly crowding forward as we made a call to respond in relationship to Jesus.

A Gold Mine

I must confess that we didn't rejoice enough when the hoards of youth came forward in Grand Forks, Dauphin, Hanover, Lumby, Nelson, Uxbridge, and Charlottetown—but we finally came to grips with the blessing. The rules "No kids on the stage" disappeared as they have led us in the party with their laughter, their fearlessness, their lack of self-consciousness.

At our next stop, Glace Bay, Nova Scotia, we saw a response from the student population that could only be described as a phenomenon. Here, where dramatic ocean waves crash against rugged shore-side cliffs, was a town in depression—the recent closure of the mines, the main industry, had the entire town of 17,000 in misery. Traditionalism and isolation prevented the numerous churches from ministering to the glaring sorrow of Glace Bay. The only real evidence of life came from the disproportionate number of high school students who wandered the streets. Warm and friendly, they welcomed us as we rolled our trailers into the vacant lot that had been their hang out. We smiled as they questioned us in those unique Cape Breton accents, closing their "o"s like Scotsmen and broadening their "a"s like Americans.

Once the Bandwagon was assembled they flocked in, skateboarding off the stage blocks and huddling in the bleachers for warmth and shelter. They were "sheep without a shepherd," 200-300 of them on the streets drinking, doing drugs, and watching street fights, looking for any relief from their boredom-plagued lives. Recognizing their own need for activity, a couple of the guys approached Russ, "Do you think we could come in here with some of our bands to 'jam' some night?" Russ immediately responded, "Sure, there's nothing happening in here 'til Sunday—you can bring everybody in tomorrow night."

To our great surprise, 150 students streamed into the Bandwagon to hear five of their own bands play an impromptu concert—complete with wailing guitars and screaming, unintelligible vocals. Each band permitted us to pray with them before they stepped to the stage; accepted our limitation that they use "clean" language in their songs; and allowed us to share between sets. And when our band mounted the stage for the finale, they all jumped to their feet to dance.

Hundreds of students hovered around the Bandwagon all week catching tidbits of the message we were serving up and the next Saturday evening, as a fight was erupting, Scott, the new Pentecostal pastor, called to the flock. "Hey, why don't you come into the Bandwagon for a minute?" To his shock 200 young people followed his lead. They sat quietly as Scott explained, "I'm the pastor of a local church filled with old people and I'm wondering why none of you are there." A cacophony of shouts and comments flew from the crowd, but he went ahead and added, "Come by our church, I'm planning concerts and drop-in activities for you." And Nate suddenly leapt to the stage, "I used to be like you guys, drinking and doing drugs because there was nothing else to do, but I've found new life in a relationship with Jesus…." When he finished they all dispersed, but conversations continued on the streets, with Upstreamers and students, until late into the night.

By the final Sunday evening, a dozen of those students had given their lives to Jesus, bushels of seed had been sown and 100 plus students sprang to the platform as we sang "Warriors," calling them to war for what is right and true in their town. Russ even prayed a prayer of commissioning over them, "God would you please use these students to bring new life and hope to Glace Bay?"

> We sat by, our mouths were shut
> Closed our eyes, giving up
> The Great One sounds the battle cry
> The hour is now, the sun is high.
>
> Come Holy fire drench the nation with
> your cleansing pow'r
> Roll like a river over me.
>
> Burn up the chaff, flood the desert with your healing balm
> O let your kingdom come.
>
> Warriors, men of peace
> When we speak, we do war!
>
> (From Warriors by Russ Rosen © 1996)

The Word Takes Root

The young have also opened doors for us—softening the hearts of resistant church people; tearing down the "you-must-be-silent-in-church" pressure that can inhibit families; leading apprehensive parents in to hear the Gospel. The single mom from across the street in Hanover, Ontario, (June 1998) was dragged to the Bandwagon by her rambunctious kids—they were the ones scrambling onto the stage or screaming around on their bikes. One day she confided with a team member, "I'm headed into a custody battle for the kids and I'm terrified of losing them." We committed to pray and she came to us on the day custody was denied, emotionally overwhelmed, and prepared to finally resign her confused life to Jesus.

Change for the Next Generation

The young have also been the planting of something new for the generations of the future. Our project in the tiny community of Rock

Creek, British Columbia (spring 1997), was another one of those difficult times when attendance was slim. But undaunted, Ralph, a local pastor, kept on with a burning vision to reach the Spanish students he had been developing relationships with in a nearby commune in the mountains. These mysterious students immigrated to Canada where Spanish adults had established a community of quality education, training in Spanish dance, and music as a way of life. Ralph invited them to the Bandwagon to share their dance and music with us and quickly friendships grew. By the end of the week, popping in for the tail end of a program, several of them committed their lives to Jesus.

Later that week when the newspapers reported a Spanish prostitution ring, which was laundering money through a Canadian commune, we knew that there had been a purpose. Those students, clearly unaware of any subversive activities that the adults were involved in, had been singled out and humiliated. We assured them of our friendship and prayed that the spiritual seeds deposited would be the planting of something new for this next generation.

We Need Each Other

Unlike other cultures, North America has generally kept the generations separated—we don't know, understand, or honor one another inter-generationally. One of the blessings for my children, therefore, has been that this traveling community, ranging in age from newborn to middle age, have become their friends, family, fellowship, advocates, mentors. Not always an easy undertaking, but still a blessing.

The greatest challenge was before my husband, Russ—fueled by drive and vision to make something successful of the Bandwagon project, he was inclined to stride ahead and set things in motion, whether or not the family is yet in step with him. Russ had a dream that gave him new perspective. In it he saw a swimming race involving families. As the starting gun went off, many of the men lurched forward and took a quick lead, but their despairing families were struggling to keep up; mothers were swimming with babies and trying to keep other little ones afloat. Russ saw that the men, who were pausing to help their families, though lagging behind the other men, caused their whole family to finish the race. An obvious strategy to me, but a revelation to Russ—he needed to slow down and let the pace of his family determine his pace. The effects on our children have been encouraging. They have become ministers in their own right.

Our youngest, Bethany, even as a very young toddler, would fearlessly step up to the stage as the music began each evening—a lone tiny figure in the center of an empty platform, oblivious of the stares and benevolent chuckles from the crowd. Her unaffected liberty and joy always set an atmosphere of freedom.

Tadia was 10 years old when we were in Hanover, Ontario (June 1998). She had quickly gathered a group of neighborhood kids together and she would regularly lead off to the store to buy candy with her own savings. Each evening after the Bandwagon program, Tadia took it upon herself to walk Amber (one of her new best friends) home, and one afternoon Amber's pain finally spilled out. She and her siblings lived with their mom and her angry boyfriend, who treated the kids badly. Tadia was at a loss about how to comfort her friend's grief, but she knew that Amber needed Jesus. Tadia called me over and together we prayed for Amber—before long she had responded to Jesus and accepted a new life in Him.

On the very first day in Cowansville, Québec (June 1999), Bethany, then age 3, struck up a quick friendship with 9-year-old Carol Ann, who was French. (Bethany always accurately rolled the "r" of in Car-r-rol in the distinct French manner. Too cute.) Though they couldn't speak each other's languages, Bethany would come to the door saying, "Car-r-rol Ann wants me to go swimming" or "Can I go get ice cream with Car-r-rol Ann?" If asked how she knew what Carol Ann was saying, she'd respond, "I dunno." At the Bandwagon, Carol Ann was the first one there, dancing up a storm with Bethany, laughing uncontrollably at the clowns, listening for as long as possible before her mother hauled her off to get ready for bed—sometimes arriving again, in her pajamas, to get in some last bits of fun. Thanks to the love of little Bethany, seeds were being sown in Carol Ann's life.

And the Least

In addition to the children, there have been others, the "least" of our society, who have been an unexpected expression of God's blessing. Henri Nouwen, in his book *Lifesigns* says, "The intimacy of the house of love always leads to solidarity with the weak. The closer we come to the heart of the One who loves us with an unconditional love, the closer we come to each other in the solidarity of a redeemed humanity."[1]

Jonathan, a boy with Down's syndrome, mounted the stage one evening with a group of other people desiring prayer from the team, but none of us could understand his slurring, incomprehensible words. With a patronizing flurry we encouraged him to move out of the path of our ministering, but he persisted until we allowed him to testify—we all panicked. He's going to destroy the delicate spiritual "mood" we had worked all evening to create. God knew better. We reluctantly yielded and held the microphone to his stammering mouth. Suddenly Christie grasped another microphone, and word-by-word began to bring the interpretation of the tongue. "God loves us," he slurred, "God wants us to love Him…, but we do bad things," the speaker and his translator shared. "I thank God that He loves me…". The place was silenced by the impact of his words—God was speaking—our neglectful, ungrateful hearts were being challenged by this unlikely prophet.

Melissa, a young Down's syndrome woman, danced so exuberantly to our music, I must confess, she brought a few giggles. But her worship was sincere and her faith meaningful as she came forward to be baptized. Her mother told us that she had secretly baptized Melissa's siblings because her husband was "anti-God," but she had never baptized Melissa. Melissa's mother, so moved by the witness of her daughter's faith, decided to rededicate her life as well.

Feasting at the Table of the Lord

The story of the wedding feast (see Matthew 22) is our signpost: those who are busy with the many important demands of life will miss the call to God's feast, but the blind and the lame and the poor won't. This ongoing lesson has stood out to us on the nights when it seemed that the only ones who heard the message were the *least* of who we wanted to hear it. Yet, they were the first to accept it with joy.

That was not my understanding on the night an inebriated man cornered me in the Bandwagon. I was fearful and apprehensive of this disheveled specimen of humanity. Teeth blackened with chewing tobacco; hair wildly askew; deep-set eyes lurking beneath a jutting brow; an unkempt beard playing havoc with his chin; too-small-clothes accentuating his hulking 6 and a half foot frame, and bared feet scarred and calloused—George was intimidating to say the least. He kept spouting at me in his drunken slur, "I need to talk to you, it's-s-s-really important!" I eluded him just long enough to push Justyn in his direction.

What did he want? To be baptized. Truly. Justyn wisely put him off until the next evening to make sure that he was serious and sober, but George arrived on time and in his right mind, ready to take the plunge. He was miraculously coherent as he shared in hushed tones, "I accepted Jesus into my life years ago, but today I want to turn my life around and return to Him." Both he and his equally struggling friend, Gary, were baptized that night and came back each subsequent night to the Bandwagon, demonstrating, by their sobriety and faithfulness, the work that God was doing in their lives.

Upside-down Kingdom

God is teaching us the true nature of His Kingdom. Jesus said it time and time again, *"The kingdom of God is like this…"*—not what we think it should be. It is a spreading tree that grew from a tiny seed (see Matthew 13:32). It is a treasure hidden (see Matthew 13:44). It is a merchant who sells everything for one valuable pearl (see Matthew 13:46). It is a landowner who believes: *"the last will be first and the first will be last"* (Matthew 20:16). It is a banquet not to missed (see Matthew 22:2).

To look at our world through His eyes of love and compassion is to align ourselves with His upside-down Kingdom. We need to take note lest we make the same mistakes that others have made: trodding on the tiny seeds of children because they don't yet look like a spreading tree; missing the treasure of the disabled because the prize is hidden; not purchasing the pearl of a broken life because it costs us too much to acquire. To recognize the last and the least is to recognize who is precious in the Kingdom and, in this, to enjoy the celebration of the banquet with the King.

Endnote

1. Henri J.M. Nouwen, *Lifesigns* (Darton Longman & Todd, Ltd., and Doubleday & Company, Inc., 1966), 51.

CHAPTER 18

God in the Rearview Mirror

I am not an adventurer at heart—I share my father's disdain for the cold; I love the comfort of life indoors; I am terrified of ocean waters; I love safety and predictability, not risk. So I was in awe, as I watched the movie footage of the discovery of the "Northwest Passage" by Henry Larsen in his ship, the St. Roch (pronounced "rock"). The famed Northwest Passage was one of the last frontiers of discovery on the Americas and called a formidable challenge to adventurers who might risk life for success. His task was to chart a shipping route through the frozen wilderness that lay north beyond the Canadian territories—many had attempted the trek and returned in despair, or died in the effort, leaving only a trail of decaying bodies and frozen remnants of the struggle.

The aging footage and the first-hand chronicle of the voyage are etched in my mind—mountains of ice, frigid waters, and stark, white landscape, all accentuating the dramatic tale of how aspirations of greatness had been reduced to a battle for survival. I was gripped by tales of the St. Roch frozen in the ice, unable to advance; of the crew desperately struggling for warmth, food and shelter; of frostbite, amputation, and death.

But the most riveting commentary came from the captain's account of one terrifying day (my paraphrase):

> "There before our ship was a wall of ice so enormous there was nothing else in view. Behind us a forceful stream of ice floes rushed us forward. Our abrupt conclusion was that our Maker had ordained our end—that in seconds we were to be smashed to bits on the gigantic mountain of glass. On board, two Eskimo guests began to sing loudly. When asked what they were doing, they replied, 'We are praying for the white man's God to save us'." At the moment the floes pressed us to our fate, a tiny space appeared in the ice wall, and then opened to an enormous route of escape and we sailed clear."[1]

For some very odd reason, I began to cry. It was how I had always felt about the task of trying to reach the nation with the love of God—it was a huge, impenetrable mountain of ice that no one could possibly get through. The force of the Spirit seemed to be prodding us forward, but there seemed to be no means by which to successfully accomplish the assignment. It was hopeless.

In that moment, those years ago, before we ever considered a national trek, God seemed to be speaking through all of those lies, "Keep on advancing, I will open a way." In these five years since we have been seeing it. Mountain after mountain of obstacles was removed for the advance of the Kingdom of God in the nation—mountains of financial inability torn down; mountains of resource obstacles destroyed; mountains of resistance to the message crushed; mountains of division knocked out; mountains of human limitation surmounted.

The Rock

Yet as we headed into the last months of our journey, there was one mountain not allowing our advance—"The Rock," Newfoundland. While the team was still in Summerside, Prince Edward Island (September 1999), Bruce and Donna, our "ahead team," traveled to this last province to pull together our mission there. We had in mind that Newfoundland would host huge stadium events in celebration of our feat of crossing the nation. "Surely," we concluded, "the momentum we've picked up will spill over into this final province and the place will rise up to celebrate with us." Again, we presumed wrongly. Bruce and Donna returned calls week after week, lamenting, "Nothing is opening up. No one wants us here."

With only three months left, we began to intercede for God's purposes to prevail as we proceeded toward the most eastern part of the nation. On one afternoon we sat together, lingering in half-hearted prayer—the difficulties of Summerside and of Newfoundland were not what we had anticipated at this point in the journey. A pat on the back and a, "Well-done-good-and-faithful-servant" commendation is what we were hoping to hear, complete with a, "It's-okay-you-can-go-home-now" consolation. But God had an entirely different closure in mind, and as we prayed He was faithful to speak it.

Someone had a vision of a huge rock with a lobster on it—was there a connection between Summerside (a lobster town) and our Newfoundland dilemma (the "rock")? The hard exterior of the lobster shell and the soft interior suggested that if we were to get through the hard stuff, we would find the good stuff. Someone else got a picture of a group of vagabonds traveling through barren streets, no one welcoming them, but as they keep pushing on doors, one pushed the right door and they are suddenly caught up in a whirlwind that carries them to the top of a high-rise building. There, they begin to dance and celebrate. Unsure what it all meant, we pursued the next days in search of answers.

Our current project in Summerside seemed to be a hard shell—resistance, reluctance from the locals made our work difficult; hurricane warnings in this chunk of the eastern North American coastline were confirmed by a ferocious wind and rain storm that pummeled the Bandwagon and eventually ripped the tent entirely from its frame. At this point in the long journey, we were quite content to just survive it—to concede that we would put in our time on an ineffective project and carry on to the home stretch. Surely God would understand that we were tired, spent, and disheartened.

But the word came loud and clear; "The breakthrough in Summerside will be the key to the breakthrough for Newfoundland." So we pressed in, repenting for our apathy and praying for God's advance into Summerside and subsequently into Newfoundland.

The soft center was found with the children (recall Chapter 17) and in this God seemed to have cracked open the shell. But Bruce and Donna continued to call us reporting that there were still no opportunities in Newfoundland—the breakthrough wasn't coming. We persisted, plodding along to our next destination, Glace Bay. It was no small coincidence that this place, too, was a lobster town and our interaction with the youth would again be the "good stuff" in the center of the project.

Meanwhile, Bruce and Donna were frantically pushing on doors and none were budging. Overwhelmed, Bruce sat one day in the office of one of the local pastors and finally poured out his heart, "I am gripped with grief because I have this wonderful team, with a wonderful message ready to come here in a couple of weeks but there is resistance. Why?" The pastor caught the tone of hopelessness in Bruce's voice and immediately called in his intercessors to pray for the team and for God's purposes.

Keep Advancing

Back in Glace Bay, we were connecting with the students, and were helping the churches of the community work together for the first time. People were being encouraged and inspired to let God bring about the changes that would transform the town into a place of hope and vision. Even the mayor dropped in to say so. It seemed to be no surprise that immediately on the heels of the powerful work going on in Glace Bay came the breakthrough into Newfoundland. Within a week, to Bruce and Donna's joy and relief, the projects there burst open. Leaving the Bandwagon rigs behind, we sailed with our motorhomes, trailers and vans, in the chill of late October, to the shores of blessèd Newfoundland. The end was in sight!

But this was not to be a simple dénouement to our travel story. Newfoundland is called "the Rock" for some very good reasons. Geographically, it is a healthy chunk of land located all alone in the open ocean between Canada and the United Kingdom. This province was its own colony of the United Kingdom until 1949, when it reluctantly joined the Confederation of Canada. Newfoundland's main city is a grueling 16-hour ferry ride from Canada's mainland and has been settled for hundreds of years longer than any other place in the nation.

Economically, Newfoundland has gone through unequaled peaks and tumbles, but has always gritted through to victorious survival. Environmentally, the rugged terrain and the unyielding climate of rain and cold have punished these island dwellers incessantly—loss is a fact of life here. Linguistically, they have a banter that is as fascinating as it is entertaining. Is it any wonder that before descending on the place, we heard the comment, "If you think that Québec is a distinct society, wait 'til you get to Newfoundland!" Out of simple necessity these people are experts at being hearty and stubborn and on "the Rock" they are strengthening that skill.

The Gap in the Wall

Had we taken to heart the warnings, we would have allocated the appropriate time, as we had in Québec, to properly understand this unique culture, but we were tired, maybe over-confident. People were polite in receiving us, but the Newfoundlanders didn't seem to click with our message or our way of conveying things. They didn't even seem to enjoy our music. In persistent determination the Spirit pushed us on through a little gap in the mountain of ice.

The breakthrough: our key theme, reconciliation. The rock of the Newfoundland heart resided on a foundation of three prominent divisions: between the outports ("Baymen") and the city ("Townies"); between Church denominations; and between themselves (once a Newfoundlander, always a Newfoundlander) and the rest of Canada ("from away"). Their laughter gave way to tears one evening, as numerous people responded to God's call to turn from their divisions. "We needed to hear this," one woman shared. "We manage to protect ourselves by our hardness of heart—it's how we cope with the difficult things that life throws our way—but it has kept us from the love of God. Today we want God to heal us."

God was imploring the people of "the Rock" to turn from depending on the strength of their land, on the strength of their will, on the strength of their culture, to depending on Jesus, The Rock. How true for the rest of the nation too—He is the foundation on which we stand. As His ambassadors we are:

> *A voice of one calling: 'In the desert prepare the way for the Lord, make straight in the wilderness a highway for our God. Every valley will be raised up, every mountain and hill made low; the rough ground shall become level, the rugged places a plain. And the glory of the Lord will be revealed, and all mankind together will see it.' For the mouth of the Lord has spoken* (Isaiah 40:3-5).

And He continues to say to us, "The way is clear, now go, and take the nation."

The Finale

The damp snow of Newfoundland's late November escorted our entourage westward down the Number One highway. Relief, sadness, and exhaustion surrendered us to numbed emotions. Twelve of the original fifteen team members had finished the whole journey - some 70 people in total had jumped on and off the Bandwagon over the course of the 5 years. Our three daughters were intent on one thing: Christmas at home in British Columbia—now 7,000 kilometers (4,350 miles) away! My mind was whirring with thoughts. *What had we just done? Did anything happen? Why did our last project seem to finish with a fizzle? Where was God in all this?*

I can make sense of it only in retrospect. In the way that five years of travel were completed in the reverse direction in just a couple of weeks, so a whole lifetime of the experience can feasibly be sandwiched between the covers of a book—but the fullness of the journey can't. It has been in the time of chewing on and ingesting the events, the struggles, and our enduring relationship with the Almighty God, that greater understanding comes. Presumably, more and deeper as the years roll by.

As I remember the events of our national trek, God appears to poke His head out of the memory to point out, "There I was…that was where I directed you to go…this is what I had for you to do." A simple glance in my rearview mirror lets me see His face in the experiences of the past and reassures me in those times when I'm at a loss to comprehend: "Was all of it worth the grief and the expense (personal and financial)?"

God Comforts Me With…

> *The fruit of righteousness will be peace; the effect of righteousness will be quietness and confidence forever. My people will live in peaceful dwelling places, in secure homes, in undisturbed places of rest. Though hail flattens the forest and the city is leveled*

completely, how blessed you will be, sowing your seed by every stream... (Isaiah 32:17-20a).

What has been temporary discomfort to me, I know has far-reaching effect for the generations of the future—we have been part of paving the road of righteousness for our children's children and beyond. Unseen seeds, perhaps, but by the grace of God, it will become a fertile field bursting with the love of God and restoring this nation as a dwelling place for His very Presence.

And even beyond all this, there has been more. Ultimately, God has been drawing each of us close to Himself. He has been making a point of revolutionizing my understanding and transforming me. Because He loves me. Because He wants me to learn to love Him more. Because He wants me to let go of attitudes and behaviors that weren't good for me. Because He wants me to trust Him more. Because the more time I spend with Him, the more I realize that He is my very great reward.

Endnote

1. Henry A. Harson, Frank R. Sheer, Edvard Omholt-Jensen, *The Big Ship*, (Toronto, ON: McClelland Steward Ltd., 1967).

APPENDIX

Schedule of Events

We welcome you to travel through the land with us through this brief synopsis of our pilgrimage:

1995

July: Aldergrove, British Columbia (BC)
August: White Rock, BC
September: Powell River, BC
October: Campbell River, BC
December: Kyuquot, Tahsis & Zeballos, BC

1996

February-March: 6-week tour of the prairies
April: Fort Langley, British Columbia (BC)
May: Walnut Grove (Langley), BC
June-July: Abbotsford, BC
July-August: Penticton, BC

September: Vernon, BC & Lumby, BC
October: Nelson, BC

1997

February: Another tour of the prairies
March: Grand Forks, Greenwood, Rock Creek, BC
April: Brief weekend in Calgary, Alberta
May: Lloydminster, Alberta
June: North Battleford, Saskatchewan (SK)
July: Swift Current, SK
August: Moose Jaw, SK
September: Dauphin, Manitoba (MB)
October: Portage La Prairie, MB
December: Winnipeg, MB

1998

January: Kenora, Ontario (ON)
February: Thunder Bay, ON
March: Sault Ste. Marie, ON
April: Pre-mission tour of Ontario
May: Waterloo, ON
May/June: Hanover, ON
June: Orangeville, ON
July: Lindsay, ON
August: Peterborough, ON
September: Hamilton, ON
October: Uxbridge, ON
November: MFJ album in Morin Heights, Québec (QC)

1999

February-March: Pre-mission work in Québec (QC)
April: Aylmer, Gatineau & Hull, QC
May: Laval, QC
June: Cowansville, QC

Schedule of Events

July: Quispamsis & St. George, New Brunswick (NS)
August: Grand Bay, NB & Truro, NS
September: Charlottetown & Summerside, Prince Edward Island (PEI)
October: Glace Bay, Cape Breton, NS
November: Clarenville & St. John's, New Foundland

Thanks be to God! He gives us the victory through our Lord Jesus Christ (1 Corinthians 15:57).

Contact the Author

Sandy Rosen
Box 281
Fort Langley, BC
V1M 2R6 Canada
www.sandyrosen.com

For music references go to:
www.russrosenband.com

For photos of the journey go to:
www.upstream.ca

Books to help you grow strong in Jesus

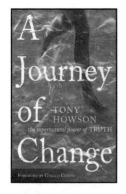

A Journey of Change
The supernatural Power of Truth

By Tony Howson

When is Truth not The Truth?

Experiencing the Spirit of Truth opens your life to incredible fullness in God. Allowing the Spirit of Truth to guide your life and influence your decisions will lead you into an exciting new realm of joy and purpose.

"And you shall know the truth, and the truth shall set you free" (John 8:32).

Learn the difference between:

* Truth and Holy Spirit Truth.
* A then experience and a now experience.
* Saul and Paul.
* A suddenly and a dead tradition.
* Right and wrong.

Experience the Spirit of Truth today—and everyday—through your personal Comforter, the Holy Spirit.

ISBN:88-89127-33-3

Order Now from Destiny Image Europe
Telephone: +39 085 4716623 - Fax +39 085 4716622
E-mail: ordini@eurodestinyimage.com

Internet: www.eurodestinyimage.com

Books to help you grow strong in Jesus

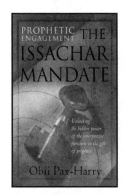

PROPHETIC ENGAGEMENT,
THE ISSACHAR MANDATE

Unlocking the hidden power of the interpretive function in the gift of prophecy

By Obii-Pax-Harry

And this Gospel of the Kingdom shall be preached in all the world for a witness unto all nations; and then shall the end come (Matthew 24:14).

Now is the time to reach out and share God with the world. Using the gifts He gave you will bring about His purpose in your life—and the Church as a whole.

Prophetic Engagement is a "clarion call" to the prophetic church to:

*   Reposition the gift of prophecy to an interpretative role.
*   Engage more proactively with Christian media.
*   Serve the unsaved world with divine abilities granted by God.
*   Establish an apostolic and prophetic Christian media army.
*   Set firm foundations so the house of God can stand as designed.

Learn today how you can move the Gospel forward!

ISBN:88-89127-31-7

Order Now from Destiny Image Europe
Telephone: +39 085 4716623 - Fax +39 085 4716622
E-mail: ordini@eurodestinyimage.com
Internet: www.eurodestinyimage.com

Additional copies of this book and
other book titles from
DESTINY IMAGE EUROPE
are available at your local bookstore.

We are adding new titles every month!

To view our complete catalog on-line, visit us at:

www.eurodestinyimage.com

Send a request for a catalog to:

Via Acquacorrente, 6
65123 - Pescara - ITALY
Tel. +39 085 4716623 - Fax +39 085 4716622

* *

Are you an author?

Do you have a "today" God-given message?

CONTACT US

We will be happy to review your
manuscript for a possible publishing:

publisher@eurodestinyimage.com